PORT OF NEW YORK.

TERMINAL FACILITIES

MORDECAI.

Fowler Lummis
Philad'a
1886.

A REPORT

ON THE

TERMINAL FACILITIES FOR HANDLING FREIGHT

OF THE

Railroads Entering the Port of New York:

ESPECIALLY OF THOSE RAILROADS HAVING DIRECT

WESTERN CONNECTIONS.

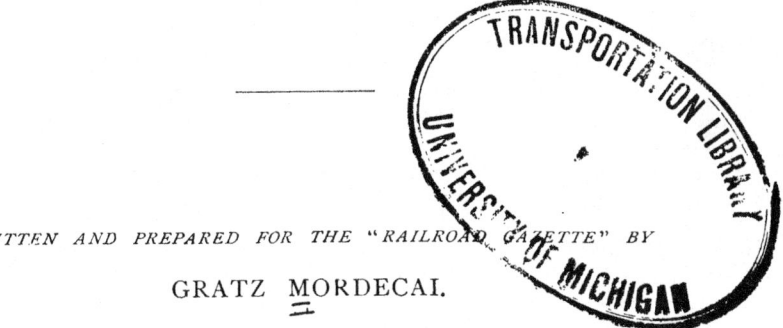

'TTEN AND PREPARED FOR THE "RAILROAD GAZETTE" BY

GRATZ MORDECAI.

NEW YORK:
RAILROAD GAZETTE.
73 Broadway.
1885.

Transportation
Library
TF
308
.N5
M8

Copyrighted, 1885, by GRATZ MORDECAI.

RAILROAD TERMINAL FACILITIES

FOR

Handling Freight at the Port of New York.

INTRODUCTION.

It is evident that the work of moving freight on railroads consists in general of the operations of transporting or hauling, which may be classed as "Work on the Road and at Division Yards," and also of the operations of handling, or receiving and delivering, which may be classed as "Work at Stations and Station Yards." And it is equally evident that these two classes of work are distinct both in methods of operation and management, for while the railroad companies have full control of all details of hauling, the work of handling directly depends also upon the merchants, and their commercial laws and business methods.

This division is not always clearly defined, either in railroad work or accounts, but it is proposed herewith to make a distinct separation and to give some notes on the terminal work alone of some of the railroads entering the port of New York. It is not intended to give complete details, but simply to give an idea of the general methods; of the appliances used and the work done. Very little description will be given of the clerical work, and none at all of the management.

The freight handled by these railroad companies has been divided into three general commercial classes:

Goods for local use and local storage: The terminal movement of this class is east-bound, and is from the cars to the stores, markets, warehouses and factories, which last are generally situated inland in New York, and on the water in Brooklyn and other points.

Goods sold in New York for shipment to the interior: The

terminal movement of this class is west-bound, and is from the warehouses and factories to the cars.

Goods for direct export or import to other markets : The terminal movement of this class is both east-bound and west-bound, and is between the vessels and the cars.

It should be remembered, however, that this terminal movement in general is not always either direct or prompt, even where the railroad tracks run to the warehouses and shipping docks. The goods in general, whilst in the hands of the railroad companies, are subject to the important operations of weighing and inspection by the merchants, the commercial exchanges, and the railroad companies themselves, and in addition to this the final destination of the east-bound freight is often uncertain. Hence the railroad companies are frequently obliged to furnish room for temporary storage in their freight houses, and it will therefore be well before giving any details of operation to divide the freight handled at stations and yards into the following terminal classes :

Class I.—Goods promptly handled in large lots and weighed, either in the car by the railroads or in piece by the merchants, such as machinery, lumber, coal, etc., both in-bound and out-bound. The handling of this freight is a mere transfer to and from the cars, often performed by the merchants, and on account of the simplicity of this operation requires but a small expenditure of room and labor. It is more open to the application of mechanical contrivances, and it is the constant effort of all railroad companies to enlarge the limits of this class of operations.

Class II.—Goods promptly handled, but requiring weighing by the piece and sorting for destination by the railroad companies, such as dry goods, groceries and other out-bound freight. The handling of this freight requires more room and labor than the first class, and any system of work or communication between the railroads and the shippers by which the labor on this class of operations can be diminished is worthy of consideration

Class III.—Goods not promptly handled and requiring temporary storage on account of inspection or uncertain destination, such as grain, flour and other in-bound freight. The handling of this freight requires much more room and labor than any other, and machinery is applied to it as far as possible.

The hauling in this city is not done by the merchants except in a few cases, and never by the railroad companies, but by third parties, who own the drays and horses and contract for the work at a fixed price per piece or per ton, according to the freight. The drays hold from 3 to 4 tons of heavy freight for each 2-horse team.

It is possible that the following description may suggest standard arrangements of both freight house and yards, and also help to fix the approximate area necessary for the daily movement of a given number of cars at country, city and seaport stations.

Terminal Works and Business of the New York Central & Hudson River Railroad.

The general business of this road extends over connecting lines to all parts of the Western states and Canada, and the railroad proper with its branches traverses for a long distance a portion of New York state, having a great variety of products and a rich and enterprising population.

The Western freight business, known as the "Line Freight," is managed by the following companies and organized agencies, each using special cars, viz: Merchants' Dispatch Transportation Company, doing certain business over all connecting lines; the Blue Line on the Michigan Central Railroad; the Canada Southern Line over the Michigan Central Railroad exclusively; the Red Line over the Lake Shore and Wabash Railroads, the Nickel Plate Line over the New York, Chicago & St. Louis Railway; the White Line over the Cleveland, Columbus, Cincinnati & Indianapolis Railway; the Midland Line over the Lake Shore and other railroads. These lines are co-operative associations of railroad companies, each road furnishing cars and receiving pay for the work in proportion to its mileage in the route.

The New York state freight business, known as "State Freight," is managed by the local agents of the railroad and its branches using New York Central & Hudson River Railroad cars.

The terminal freight stations of this road are:

The lighterage station and terminal yard at Sixtieth street, on the Hudson River.

The city stations at Thirty-third street and at Barclay street, both on the Hudson River, and the station at St. John's Park (bounded by Beach, Laight, Hudson and Varick streets) and one at Pier 5, East River.

The coal station is at Port Morris, at the entrance to Long Island Sound.

The Brooklyn station is on the Williamsburgh docks.

SIXTIETH STREET TERMINUS.—The freight tracks of this railroad enter the city by running along the east bank of the Hudson River, at the foot of a rocky bluff, until they reach Seventy-second street, about 5½ miles north of the Battery. Between Seventy-second street and Sixtieth street, where they enter and run along the city street (Eleventh avenue), the tracks, still following the foot of a rocky bluff, skirt the lowlands which reach out to the river channel; and on this convenient site within the city limits, yet free from city streets and business, was located the principal terminal yard, with its accompanying freight docks and sheds, grain elevators and stock-yard, arranged as shown on Plate A. The site was formerly under water, and unoccupied until 1877, when Elevator A was built, and Elevator B in 1879. From that time the works were extended till 1882, when the last shed, "G," was built. The elevation of the main tracks is about 18 ft. above mean high water, and the general level of the docks and yard is 8 ft. above the same level. Hence the yard tracks have 10 ft. fall toward the river. The foot of the steepest part of this grade is shown approximately by the dotted lines on the plan. The line of the bulkhead wall follows a little west of and parallel to the line of Twelfth avenue, and the piers extend from it at an angle of 60 degrees to the southwest. At low tide the water is 16 ft. deep at the bulkhead. The total area of this property is about 57 acres, of which the piers and elevators occupy six acres, the stock-yard and abattoir 13 acres, store-house one acre, and yard 37 acres.

The original tracks leading to Elevator A were built on trestle work, but when the yard room was extended it was filled with sand brought by train from Croton, 37 miles up the river. Some ashes and city refuse were used in the northern part of the yard and also back of the bulkhead. The tracks are of good material, laid with stub switches and rail frogs. There are 22 miles of track in this yard (exclusive of the siding running north to Manhattanville, 2¾ miles), divided as shown on the plan. The bulkhead is constructed of timber crib work filled with stone, which was sunk in a trench dredged for the purpose. The cribs are about 40 ft. in height. The piers are constructed of pile bents, 7 ft. 10 in. spans centre to centre, with an extra number of piles on the north line to protect them from floating ice.

The sheds on Piers D, E and F are used for transferring east-bound freight to lighters and vessels and for temporary storage. They are two-story timber structures, sheeted with corrugated iron; the general construction of these piers and sheds is indicated on Plate B. There are no posts in the centre of the lower platform, the second story being supported by rods from the roof ; the floor joists are calculated to hold a load of 400 lbs. to the square foot.

Shed G is of different construction and is used in transferring west-bound freight from lighters and barges. It is only one-story, and the tracks are on the outside, as shown on the plan and in cross section on Plate B.

The piles for the foundation of Elevator A were driven regularly over the whole site about 2½ ft. apart, and then cut off near low water, and a platform strong enough to distribute the load laid over the whole ; from this platform stone piers were erected as supports for the posts of the timber frame-work. The outside walls of this elevator were built of brick work but slate has been substituted for it in order to diminish the load on the foundation.

Elevator B has a somewhat different foundation. The piles were driven in clusters of 25 in a space 10 × 10 and cut off about 30 ft. below the water. The stone piers to support the posts were then built on separate platforms, suspended by rods and lowered as the masonry was built. This elevator is constructed of timber frame-work sheathed with corrugated iron and slate.

Each elevator cost about $500,000.

Operation of the Yard.—East-bound Freight.—The east-bound freight train with cars for this station is switched from the main line to the siding marked "section" where the road engine leaves it, and the caboose is run to the track marked " caboose." The "section" siding extends northward about 2¾ miles and is used for the reception of trains in the busy season, but that section of the track on which the trains in general arrive only holds one train ; therefore, the cars must be quickly distributed in the yard. The way-bills are received in advance of the train, and hence the contents and destination of the cars are known, and the number of the track on which each car is to be run in the yard is at once chalked on the side of the car ; a man known as a "pin-puller" draws the pins according to the destination in the yard, and the great number of tracks allows of an excellent system of classification. Grain cars are sent on the tracks marked " grain-yard," and there are also separate tracks for other staples, as a cotton track, a tobacco track, flour tracks, and so on : thus the same kinds of freight are kept together, saving much labor in the freight house.

The yard engine is run behind the train on the section track and pushes the cars slowly forward, each section of the train as it is cut off having a brakeman to control it. The only duty of the engine is to push on its own track, for as the grade falls from each switch, the car runs to its destination without further aid. It is there coupled to the car ahead of it, so that in case of fire the yard can be quickly emptied. Each track is numbered in connection with the letter of the pier, and it is the duty of one man to take and keep in a book the position of every car from the bumper block on every track throughout the yard.

The cars can be run from the yard tracks into the freight sheds and elevators by gravity, although it takes an engine to put them in position in the elevators and at shed G.

West-bound Freight.—After the cars are unloaded on the piers, they are sorted on the tracks marked "empty yard," or in the "west-bound yard" if they are to return west empty. The empty cars are then delivered to the west-bound freight house G, first according to the general arrangement of the house, which will hereafter be shown, and then by the special orders of the foreman of the pier, according to the freight which he has to load. On account of the different lengths of the cars, it is often necessary to uncouple in order to make the doors of the cars on both tracks coincide ; hence two engines work at a time, so that as soon as a train of loaded cars is pulled out, a train of empty cars is pushed in, thus causing little delay to the men in the house. All west-bound cars from all stations are sorted on the 26 tracks marked "west-bound yard." The building of the store-house shortened the yard, so that none of the tracks hold a full train, but in other respects it is very easily operated. The cars are delivered into it by gravity, and each track is used for a special route and is designated by a number. The brakeman, as he enters this yard on a car bound for a certain track, signals the number of the track by hand signals to the three switchmen who control the yard, and the whole work is done very quietly and systematically.

In pulling up the grade out of this west-bound yard, the yard engines are obliged to assist the road engines. Trains are sent out of this yard directly for Chicago, the only further yard work being the changing of engines and cabooses on the different divisions.

Including both east-bound and west-bound, about 900 loaded cars are moved in one day, but with the same equipment 1,000 cars are frequently handled. Each car, from the time it enters the yard until it leaves to return, is moved eight times in the regular course of business.

The following is the force at work :

	Day.	Night.
Engineers	4	4
Conductors	4	4
Locomotives	4	4
Brakemen	35	35
Switchmen	28	28
Pin-pullers	4	4
Chalkers	1	1
Car record clerks	4	4
Yard-masters (assistants)	4	4
Yard-master	1	1

There is an assistant yard-master each for the east-bound, grain, and empty yards. The regular yard engine weighs about $26\frac{1}{2}$ tons, all on four drivers, the total weight, with tender loaded, being about 40 tons ; it consumes about 4 tons of coal in 24 hours.

This whole force is largely increased during the busy winter months, eight engines being sometimes in use.

Operation of the Piers in General.—Almost all the railroad business with the New York city docks, and all the business with the Brooklyn storehouses and other points in the harbor, is done by means of lighters or barges, generally holding about 450 tons. There are two lighters used by this company for quick delivery of small lots of freight, which have both steam-hoisting and propelling apparatus, but, as a general thing, the lighters are moved by separate propellers.

Ocean steamers and large vessels having regular docks do not leave them. The tracks of this railroad enter some of these docks, but, for reasons mentioned in the introduction, the movement of freight is not always direct, and even with bulk cargoes the freight is transferred by lighters. Grain is transferred from the lighters to the vessels by floating steam elevators, and miscellaneous freight by steam-hoisting apparatus, either on the vessels or on the shipping dock, where they are very general.

Independent sailing and steam vessels which have no regular docks transfer freight directly at these railroad docks, however ; hence the slips are kept to a sufficient depth for this work.

About eight years ago, before these piers were constructed, all the city lighterage was carried on at the Thirty-third street station, and the export lighterage of grain, and other " bulk" freight from Athens, about 115 miles up the river, and only 30 miles below Albany.

Operation of the East-bound Freight Piers C, D, E and F.—Pier C is out of the way, and is not used now except in case of necessity. Pier D is used for east-bound miscellaneous freight, such as provisions and manufactures, and occasionally for some west-bound freight, such as railroad iron transferred directly from vessels. Pier E, a section of which is shown on Plate B, is almost entirely devoted to export dry freight, snch as flour in sacks, and oil cake, etc. On pier F are handled barreled flour and other freight for local use or storage. All export flour is inspected on these docks, and the Produce Exchange (representing the combined merchants of the port) requires of the railroads five days' storage for this purpose. In 1883, 2,552,881 barrels of flour were brought to New York by this railroad.

On all these piers the freight is moved by hand trucks (except barrels, which are rolled on the floor), but the operation of the yard and the fact of the freight coming in large lots avoids long trucking to a considerable extent.

The second stories of the sheds on Piers D, E and F are in constant use, the freight, mostly flour, being elevated in each by six Bates automatic elevators, which are hinged sheet-iron platforms, mounted on endless iron chain belts, similar in operation to a grain elevator. As it requires an additional gang of men to handle the freight on the second floor, the first floor is used in preference. The elevators are very economical, however, and save the work of piling the freight, as the second floor more than doubles the storage area. The elevators in each house are worked by one engine of 45 horse-power, 16 × 24 in. cylinder, at about 40 lbs. pressure and 70 revolutions per minute. Each engine has an adjustable cut-off, regulating the amount of steam used to the work required. At the usual rate of speed, each elevator raises in actual practice, including the movement of the cars, 500 barrels an hour. The freight is lowered by the same contrivance, except that no steam is used ; the weight of the load carries it down, the speed being regulated by a foot brake on the second floor, and 500 barrels an hour are lowered by each leg per hour in the regular course of work. Most of the freight is moved to the lighters by hand trucks, but when the tide is low (as indicated on Plate B), the deck of the vessel is considerably below the level of the dock, and the freight is slid down a plank from the dock stick and packed by another gang of men on the lighter.

The total floor area of sheds D, E and F is 234,500 square feet, which will accommodate a daily movement of 150 cars, or about 1,500 ft. per car, which is probably equivalent to an average storage of four days.

Barreled oil is handled on the platforms between the oil tracks, the barrels being easily rolled along on top of two lines of rails laid 16 in. apart, and thus moved to and from the lighters at the bulkhead.

Export timber is transferred to lighters at the bulkhead track back of the round-house.

The coal wharf is for transferring locomotive coal from lighters.

Live stock is run directly into the stock yards; as these and the abattoir are operated by a separate company, no description will be given of them.

The tracks near the office, marked "bulk," are used for car-loads of east-bound freight, such as lumber, received for local use in this part of the city.

Organization.—East-bound Freight.—There are employed on each of the docks D, E and F one engineer (one of whom also works the steam derrick on F and G); 30 laborers, who are paid by the time worked, 17 cents an hour; two tallymen, and one clerk.

A slip is made out for each consignment in the car and checked by the tallyman as the car is unloaded; it is then sent to the main office and destination marked on it, and the goods shipped accordingly. The tallyman also records in a book the freight as it is unloaded from each car. The regular work of the men on the east-bound freight is to unload the cars and pile the freight in the house, and to load the freight stored in the house into the regular company barges. Taking both these operations into account, a good average work in ten hours is the unloading of a car of freight to each laborer, but it varies greatly according to the freight and the room in the house. Twenty-five men will unload 50 cars of oil, and taking the whole work, the average work of a man would probably be from $1\frac{1}{4}$ to $1\frac{3}{4}$ cars a day.

West-bound Freight.—The lay-out of the west-bound freight house G is shown on accompanying cut. The greater part of the work at this house is done at night, as most of the freight is collected during the day at the Brooklyn, Jersey City and New York city docks, arrives at this dock in lighters about 7 p. m., and is unloaded, sorted, weighed and loaded in cars generally before 4 o'clock in the morning, and is always on the road before 7 o'clock. The house is nicely whitewashed and admirably lit by electric lights, 30 of which are distributed around the works, the company operating its own machine on the premises.

Five regular boats run to this house every night. One boat carries line freight from the Barclay street dock; it is unloaded at doors Nos. 3 and 4. Another barge brings state and line freight from Pier 5, East River, and is unloaded at doors Nos. 1 and 2.

Another carries sugar from the Williamsburgh refinery, 2,000 barrels at a time, and is unloaded at doors Nos. 5 and 6. Another boat carries coffee from Brooklyn store-houses, and still another during the day brings miscellaneous freight from Brooklyn. There is frequently, also, a barge from the Jersey City sugar refineries. There are also a great many irregular boats from the docks and warehouses of the port, but the above are almost constant.

Lighters carrying freight which does not require weighing or sorting lie on the north side of the pier, and the freight is transferred directly over the narrow, uncovered platform. On this platform are two steam derricks, capable of handling pieces up to four tons in weight, such as barrels of soda ash and sugar, and paper stock. There are no quick-acting derricks for smaller freight, however, and that kind is unloaded by hand, unless the lighter has a steam hoist and gaff boom, in which case quick delivery can be made. Five hundred barrels an hour can be regularly raised in the last-mentioned way with one boom. Miscellaneous freight is unloaded on the south side from the barges into the house by hand trucks, which are run up to the gangways shown on the right-hand side of the plan. The lift is very variable, and at low tide men are stationed in each gangway to help the truckmen, but these additional men are afterward used in the regular gang loading the cars. The gangways coincide with the doors in the barges, and the truckmen enter the boat by one gangway and haul out by the other. The sugar boats are unloaded by rolling the barrels, and at low tide two men are necessary in the gangway to each barrel. Twenty men can unload 2,000 barrels in two hours when the tide is high, and in four hours when the tide is low.

As a general thing, the freight requiring sorting is first handled ; at the head of the incoming gangway is a switchman, who tells the truckmen at what number to put the freight, each number designating a certain place and route. After the freight is sorted it is loaded, which is done one car at a time by each gang of six men and a tallyman. The tallyman, who stands at the scales, has the duplicate shipping bills, which have been sorted in the office, and those for each car put in a separate envelope. These envelopes are indorsed, stating car, route, tallyman, etc., and when the car is loaded the envelope is taken to the office, the indorsement recorded in a book, and a memorandum way-bill made out, and all compared afterward by the man who cards the car. The duties of the tallyman are to weigh each package and put the weight and tally on the duplicate bill. He simply follows and checks the duplicate receipt ;

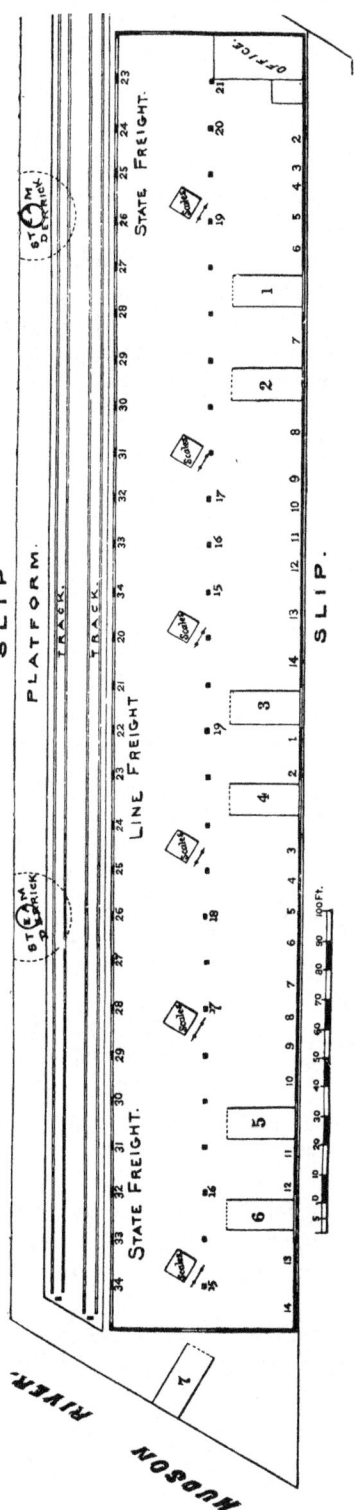

he does not make an independent record from inspection of the package, and thus avoids errors in description of the freight and works quickly, except in cases where the freight is piled so that it is hard to follow the order of the shipping bills, which is very seldom the case in this house. In handling sugar or other freight which comes in large lots, but so mixed in the loading in the barge as to require sorting, the lay-out of the house cannot be adhered to, and hence the foreman of the house instructs the yard-man how to deliver the cars.

Twenty-eight cars are loaded at a time, the north string being loaded first.

The total area of shed G is 28,600 square feet, which will accommodate a daily (12 hours) movement of 120 cars, of nearly 240 square feet per car; hence the movement of this freight is so rapid that it requires no more room to weigh and sort it than is necessary to haul it in the car.

Organization—West-bound Freight.—The night force is generally 85 laborers and 20 foremen, tallymen and clerks, and the average work is the loading of 120 cars in 10 hours. The day force is 20 men, and in 24 hours 160 cars are loaded at this pier.

The work at this pier is well arranged and concentrated. The freight comes in large barge-loads and not by the dray-load, as at city stations, and hence the men are kept steadily at a regular routine and work effectively.

Operation of the Grain Elevators.—The use of the elevator is not for the simple transfer of grain, for that work could be done by much simpler apparatus. The laws of trade require that grain be stored and weighed, and sometimes cleaned, by the railroad or allied companies, and though it is possible that the average storage is not over 10 days in length, in some cases it is extended ; hence, for a storage longer than 10 days an additional rate per bushel is charged. The great size and consequent cost of these buildings are caused, then, by a commercial necessity. Fortunately, it is found possible to apply machinery and classification to the work, and hence this great freight movement is carried on with relative economy and by a standard system, the general operation of which is well known.

Elevator A is used for handling small lots of grain and is located along the bulkhead and delivers to vessels on the river side and elevates grain from canal boats at the south end. The east and middle tracks, each holding 11 cars, are used for east-bound cars, and from them the grain is elevated. Grain to be shipped out on

BIN PLAN of ELEVATOR A.

RIVER SIDE.

— — — *Lines represent Receiving Scales & Spouts*
.... „ „ Shipping „ „

cars is loaded on the west or river track ; the grain is delivered to them by spouts running from the outside spouts which deliver to the vessels. There are eleven shipping bins on the water side, reached by the spouts from the shipping scales and also from the receiving scales, which is necessary when there is a direct transfer from the car to the vessel. The capacity of each of the scales has lately been increased to 60,000 lbs. in order to weigh a car-load, which now sometimes amounts to 50,000 lbs. The shipping bins, which are used to regulate the delivery and make it independent of the raising and weighing, are not full-sized bins. They only extend down to the height at which the spouts leave the building. The delivery from the bins on the east half of the building is made by means of the conveying belts shown, which carry the grain to the shipping elevators. These belts were originally intended to make city deliveries on the east side, but they are now run in the opposite direction. They are on a floor below the bottom of the bins and above the track. The storage capacity of Elevator A is 1,500,000 bushels.

Elevator B.—This elevator is used for large lots of grain, is located on its own pier and has 15 shipping bins on each side and 10 shipping and 10 receiving and 5 screening elevators ; these last are above the bins. Its storage capacity is 1,500,000 bushels.

Organization and Work.—Besides the Superintendent and his clerks, there are in each elevator on this track floor 1 foreman, 1 wharfmaster, 22 men with shovels (Elevator B, 20), 1 man opening cars, 1 machinery man.

Engine Room.—1 engineer, 1 fireman, day ; 1 fireman, night ; 1 oiler (boy).

Scales Floor.—1 receiving weighman, 2 shipping weighmen, 1 spoutman and helper, 1 man sweeping bins, 1 man attending shipping bins, 1 man attending screen.

Top Floor.—1 machinery man.

About 19.000,000 bushels of grain were delivered by this railroad in 1883.

Elevator A has raised 306 cars of grain in one day. The average receipts of both elevators are about 100 cars a day ; 256,000 bushels have been delivered from Elevator A in one day, and nearly as much could be done by Elevator B ; but for a week's run, taking into account the movement of the boats and other delays, 90,000 bushels for A and 80,000 bushels for B would be good work. This would require 10 tons of coal for A and about 7½ for B. The total average consumption for the year is 10 tons a day. The boilers of B furnish steam for the engines which run the elevators in sheds D and E ; the engine in shed F, the electric light engine and the steam derricks are supplied by a separate boiler using about 5 tons a day.

THIRTY-THIRD STREET TERMINUS.—The general arrangement of this yard and the adjacent freight sheds, etc., is shown on Plate A. The freight yard is on the Hudson River, 4½ miles north of the Battery and two miles south of the Sixtieth street yard. The works have grown up around the old passenger and freight station of the Hudson River Railroad, and have been enlarged as necessity required, and, as shown on the plan, the site is intersected by several city streets. There are about 26 acres in the whole property. The new piers have not yet been constructed and no plan of permanent occupation has been adopted ; hence in these respects it is a contrast to the Sixtieth street terminus. It is conveniently located as a city station for the uptown trade and a large proportion of the manufacturing districts.

A branch track at Forty-first street, about half a mile to the north, runs into a large slaughter house and pork-packing works. On the south, a double-track branch runs down Eleventh avenue to Twenty-seventh street, about a quarter of a mile, and along this branch (which is used for transferring car-load freight) are lumber yards and iron works. There is also a siding about 120 ft. long on Tenth avenue, about a mile south, just below Twelfth street and near the vegetable market, and another (half a mile further south, on West street), 3,000 ft. long, between Barrow and Spring streets, with branches into the piers of the White Star, Inman and Guion lines of transatlantic steamers.

There are about six miles of sidings in the yard and piers.

There is nothing to be noted in the construction of these piers and sheds, for, as the piers are not permanently located, the old sheds have simply been kept in running order, and such changes in the track made as found necessary. After the Manhattan Market (built by the city) was burned, this company bought the site and erected two-story brick buildings along the streets, divided by brick partitions into rooms about 60 ft. square. They have platforms on both the track and street sides. The hay sheds are wooden sheds covered with corrugated iron, open on the track side and with doors on the streets.

Operation of the Yard.—The Thirty-fourth street yard is used to distribute cars both to the sheds here and the down-town stations. The car floats running to the Barclay street pier are loaded and unloaded here, and the cars to and from the large city station at St. John's Park and the steamship docks are moved from this yard. The trains on the Hudson River division come solid for this station, the cars being arranged in the train at Albany according to destination, all the cars for each of the down-town stations being together. The road engine leaves the train at the Seventy-second street engine-house, and the Thirty-third street yard engine hauls a train of 20 cars to Thirty-third street, returning empty for another train. The details of the operation of the yard are as far as possible the same as at Sixtieth street. The yard is smaller and not arranged in a general plan, and no west-bound cars are sorted here.

The St. John's Park freight is handled on tracks marked "P," the Barclay street on "B," etc. South of this yard dummies are used, each moving 10 cars to the steamship docks and St. John's Park station.

The total force in the yard night and day each consists of four engines and 75 men, handling 250 west-bound and 325 east-bound loaded cars a day.

The 10 dummies used here are covered tank-engines, weighing about 24 tons. Six are in constant use, two working at St. John's Park, and one to the steamship docks. These latter are flagged by a boy riding on a horse in front of the train. There are 33 train-men and yard-men employed in the dummy department.

One engine is kept on east-bound trains and another on west-bound trains between this yard and the Sixtieth street yard, with seven flagmen stationed at the principal street crossings. The speed of these trains is not greater than five miles an hour.

Operation of the Freight Houses in General.—A large quantity and a great variety of local business is done at these yards, and also a considerable lighterage business in provisions and lumber. This station is conveniently located for supplies actually consumed in the city, and is near the store houses both by land and by water, whilst the down-town business consists largely of westward shipments of goods by foreign importers or commission merchants.

Pier 1 (the most southerly) is used for lighterage freight. The south platform is used largely for tobacco in hogsheads, and the north platform almost exclusively for the business of a Western firm dealing in boxed meat, transported in refrigerator cars. Their agent sells in the city, and it is delivered either for foreign export or local use. The floor area is 42,000 square feet. Sixty cars are handled here in a day, or 700 square feet per car. The average length of storage is about two days.

Pier 2.—The position of the track allows for direct transfer to lighters on the north side and to platform on the south. Lumber and provisions are mostly handled here. The floor area is 16,000 square feet. Thirty-five cars can be handled here in a day.

Pier 3 is uncovered, and is used for the direct transfer of carload lots—lumber mostly. Heavy freight is handled at the end of the pier by the ten-ton derrick, worked by hand.

Shed B.—This is for miscellaneous east-bound freight for local use. The freight is unloaded and piled in the shed till removed by the consignee. The floor area is 20,000 square feet, and 40 cars can be handled here conveniently in 12 hours, or 500 square feet per car, showing an average storage of 1½ days.

Hay shed No. 1 is for storing such hay as is not directly delivered to consignees.

Hay shed No. 2 is the regular hay market, and is leased in sections to the hay dealers, who unload their own cars. The only work required of the railroad company is to arrange the cars in the train according to the consignee's location in the shed. About 4,000 bales, or 40 cars, are handled every day, on an average, throughout the year.

Manhattan Market.—The building on Thirty-fourth street is entirely devoted to the potato business, and is operated in the same way as the hay business. The average number of cars unloaded here is 55 cars a day for the months of September, October, November and December. There are also received here during the same months about five cars of turnips and five cars of cabbage every day. On the Thirty-third street side are the dealers in beef, slaughtered and dressed in Chicago, and transported in refrigerator cars, each piece hanging from the roof. It is here run, suspended from overhead tracks, into refrigerator rooms, where it is kept till sold. They average 130 pieces of 160 lbs., or about 10 tons to a car-load.

Shed A.—This is for west-bound freight delivered by city drays. Its floor area, including the wide platform which is used for a truckway, is 10,000 square feet, on which 70 cars can be conveniently handled in 12 hours, or 150 square feet per car.

The general operation is similar to that of Pier G, Sixtieth street, except that the freight comes in dray-loads throughout the day. Car-load lots of west-bound freight are loaded directly on the cars on the "bulk" tracks. There is one six-ton hand derrick in the yard.

There are 81 laborers, checkmen, etc., employed on the east-bound freight, working 11 hours a day and handling 95 cars on the docks and in the sheds.

On west-bound freight there are 20 laborers and tallymen, handling 65 cars and working 11 hours. A large portion of this freight is loaded directly on the cars, and does not pass through the freight house.

BARCLAY STREET STATION.—This station is on the

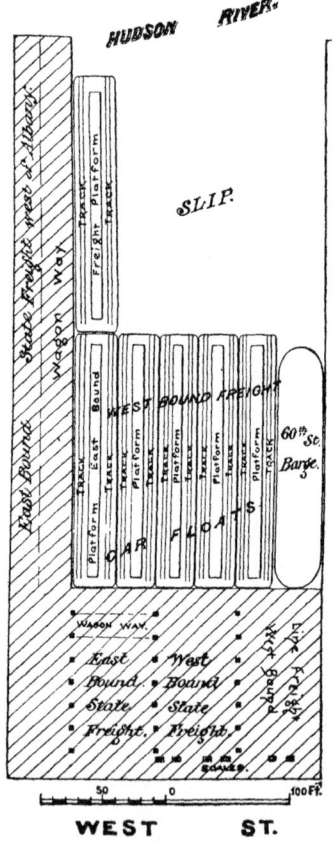

Hudson River, at the foot of Barclay street, which runs west from the Post Office. It is one mile north of the Battery. It faces on West street, and is convenient to the manufacturers, agents and storehouses in the lower part of the city.

The pier and bulkhead are covered with a wooden shed covered with corrugated iron, with a wooden lattice truss roof in 66 feet spans on bulkhead and 50 feet on pier.

Operation.—This station was established about 1878, in order to relieve the St. John's Park city station. All the way state freight west of Albany and car-loads on Hudson River Division are handled here, to and from the car floats running to Thirty-third street, and west-bound line freight is floated by barge to Pier G, Sixtieth street. The method of transporting the cars themselves to the piers on floats saves one handling, and is probably cheaper, and is certainly quicker, than to load the freight promiscuously on a barge and then unload and sort it and afterward load it on the cars.

The east-bound freight is unloaded from the floats and piled on the south side of the pier, leaving the north side for a wagon way. The freight is delivered, so far as the railroad company is concerned, when it is piled on the dock, and the consignees load and haul it. The total floor area is 60,000 square feet ; wagon way, 16,000 ; and area devoted to east-bound business, 20,000 square feet, on which 50 cars of general merchandise can be conveniently handled in a day, showing a quick average movement. Large quantities of apples are delivered here in the fall, probably 30 cars a day, and 175,000 barrels in a good season. These are transferred directly to the drays.

West-bound.—Drays with solid loads of line freight drive directly on the bulkhead and unload near the barge, the weighing and sorting being done at Pier G, Sixtieth street.

Drays having mixed freight, however, unload at the West street face, and the goods are loaded on hand trucks and immediately passed over the scales. The sorting is not done by piling on the floor ; the freight is trucked directly from the scales to the floats, where the tallymen (generally two to a float) tell the truckmen in what car to put it. The tallyman tallies on the duplicate bill sent to him from the scales.

The tracks (on the float), generally six on west-bound business, and holding 30 cars, are necessarily arranged at right angles to the receiving platforms. The advantage in operation over the usual arrangement of a platform parallel to and on the side of the track is as follows : In a large city, where goods are sent to, say, 60 different stations and routes, it is often impossible, on account of want of room in freight house and yard, to lay out a platform on a fixed arrangement, and work both drays and cars in harmony, in order to attain the best theoretical arrangement of the dray unloading opposite its proper car. Even if this arrangement is attempted, it would not allow for a dray-load of goods mixed in destination, which necessarily occurs in using the large drays of New York. By the arrangement we are now considering, however, the freight is immediately weighed and trucked in one direction, and with only one handling, into the car.

The disadvantage is the long haul, averaging 250 ft., with an average load of about 200 lbs. to the man. Only a certain number of men can work to advantage, and in busy times the goods are not trucked away as fast as unloaded from the drays, and hence there is delay and a blockade of drays.

One way to avoid this is, first, to take a short haul and sort and pile the freight in the bulkhead shed, and then take the long haul to the floats afterward, which is done at some piers. If any sort of machinery could be used to do the long hauling, this arrangement of freight house might be applied with advantage in other circumstances. It would be, however, a mixture of machine and hand labor, which might be difficult to regulate, and even after the goods were thoroughly sorted, on account of the tallying and loading, probably only one car could be loaded at a time. To be sure, the varying heights of the floats caused by the rising and falling of the tides would make it more complicated to apply such machinery here, even if it were practicable otherwise ; and it could certainly best be applied economically at stations exclusively devoted to freight moving in one direction.

The average force at work is :

14 clerks.

24 tallymen, weighmen, etc.

40 truckmen, 11 hours a day.

Handling :

30 cars east.

30 cars west.

Though in the busy times, as in the apple season, there are 90 laborers and 70 cars of east-bound freight and 50 west-bound.

PIER 5—*FREIGHT STATION*.—This consists of three piers about 60 ft. wide and 400 ft. long, situated on the East River, a quarter of a mile north of the Battery. It is mostly used for flour, the railroad depots for which are generally in this neighborhood.

Pier 5 is covered with an ordinary wooden shed, built in 16 ft. sections, with a door in alternate sections. The barrels are occasionally piled five tiers high, though this brings a heavy weight on the bottom barrels ; there is then a distributed load of 280 lbs. per square foot of floor.

Operation— West-Bound.—Pier 4 (uncovered) is generally used simply as a wharf for a barge. The drays are unloaded directly into the barge which runs to pier G, Sixtieth street. The business is miscellaneous freight, and amounts sometimes to 200 tons a day.

East-Bound.—The Produce Exchange requires the railroad to give five days' storage for flour for inspection ; this is done for local trade, mostly at this station, where it comes in barges from Sixtieth street station, for city and Brooklyn delivery to merchants, bakers, etc. It changes hands on this wharf, and its average length of storage is five days. The necessary handling is done by rolling the barrel on the floor, one man to a barrel. The barges are unloaded by railroad workmen, but the city drays are loaded by the drivers and longshoremen. Eighteen thousand barrels have been on this wharf at one time on 34,000 square feet, neglecting the wagon way of 8,000 square feet.

Pier 6 is uncovered and used mostly for handling flour, which is protected when necessary by tarpaulins.

STEAMSHIP DOCKS.—Single-track branches run into the docks of the White Star, Inman and Guion lines. They are on the Hudson River, facing West street, about two miles north of the Battery and two miles south of the Thirty-third street yard. The business is mostly east-bound freight, largely cheese and provisions, consigned for direct-export. During the busy season the business amounts to 20 cars a day for each line.

ST. JOHN'S PARK—FREIGHT STATION.—This is shown on accompanying cut, and is situated in the city about 1,200 ft. from the Hudson River, 2½ miles south of Thirty-third street yard, 4½ miles south of Sixtieth street, and 1½ miles north of the Battery. It is conveniently located for the dry-goods and grocery trades, and is the principal shipping point of west-bound freight from the jobbers.

It occupies the site of a former private park, and is surrounded by streets about 80 ft. in width. The tracks enter it on curves of about 160 ft. radius ; there is one short siding on Hudson street, but no yard. The building was erected in 1868. It occupies four acres, and has 0.6 mile of track, or eight tracks capable of holding 12 cars apiece, making a total of 96 cars inside. The tracks occupy 36,000 square feet ; driveways, 27,000 square feet.

The foundations of the walls are stone masonry and concrete;

the foundations of the posts are separate piers, in some cases 16 ft. deep. It is a three-story fire-proof building of brick walls, iron columns and beams, and flooring of brick arches, of 3 ft. spans. The second and third floors are used as a general warehouse. The door sills for receiving and delivering from drays are 27 in. above

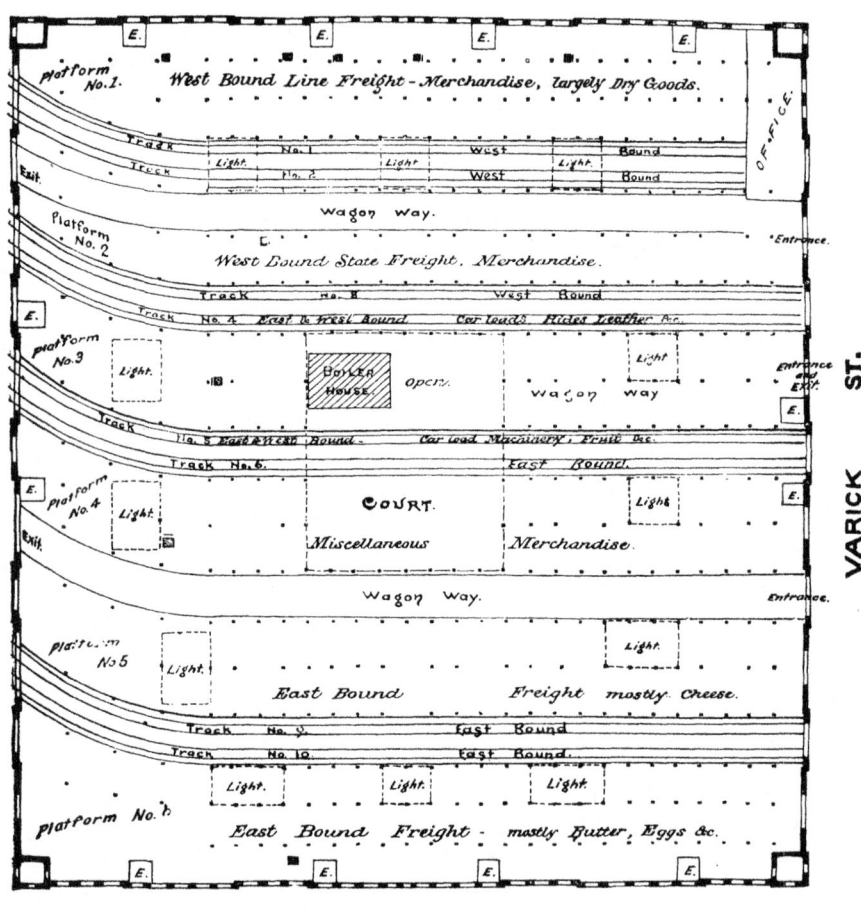

the street, and the track platforms are 3 ft. 9 in. high above the top of rail, which will allow of the opening of a hinged door to a refrigerator car. The light comes from openings indicated by the dotted lines. At night it is lit by gas. The doors are iron and fold vertically, entering a recess in the jamb. They are 6 ft. 6 in. wide. The building was originally constructed to allow the wagons to enter and load and unload directly from the platforms, but two tracks were subsequently removed, and the house arranged as shown. No. 1 platform is paved with wooden blocks like a wooden pavement. Platform No. 2 is plank. Platform No. 3 is paved with stone blocks, and teams drive in on it, leaving by the same door they enter. Platform No. 4 is also stone blocks. Platforms 5 and 6 are plank.

Operation.—East-bound.—The loaded cars, which are brought from Thirty-third street, are arranged in the train according to the destination in the house, and run into the house by two dummies kept at this station. As soon as freight arrives in the station, messengers are sent to notify consignees through the business part of the city south of Houston street. The drayman goes to the office and is told on what platform he can find his freight, and gets a pass which admits him to the building. The delivery clerk (whose duty it is to note where each car is unloaded on the platform) delivers the goods and gets a receipt in a book. As each car is unloaded the contents are recorded in a book by a checkman.

Platform No. 6 is largely used for small farm produce—butter, eggs, etc.

Platform No. 5 is mostly used for cheese. This comes consigned to commission merchants who have no ware-rooms, hence the cheese changes hands on this platform. That which is sold for export is repacked and branded. A large quantity is also sent to what are known as cold stores, some of which are in the building. They are here operated by condensing anhydrous ammonia by steam engines to about 150 lbs. pressure, and then letting it expand in pipes through the building. The refrigerator rooms are thus kept at different temperatures, ranging down to 20 degrees and even lower. The work on these platforms, 5 and 6, takes 400 square feet per car-load a day.

Platform No. 3 is for both east and west-bound car-load freight—machinery, fruit, hides, leather, etc. As there is no storage room for cars, this movement must be prompt, and it consignees do not unload the cars they are returned to Thirty-third street. The drays drive directly to the car.

Platform No. 4 is used in handling general merchandise, mostly manufactures.

West-bound Freight.—Platforms Nos. 1 and 2 are laid out as shown. The drays with freight for this station form into a long line down Laight to Canal street, along Canal to West Broadway, and then up South Fifth avenue, and as places are opened at the freight house they unload the freight on the platform. No drays are allowed to join the line after 5 P. M., and there are generally 80 left in line at that time during the busy season. The only classification made by the draymen is that they are obliged to unload "line" freight on Platform No. 1, and "state" freight south of Albany on Platform No. 2. As the goods are unloaded at the most convenient place for the draymen, they are sorted for distribution after being weighed. The weighman tells the truckman the number of the column at which he is to leave the package, and it is loaded on the cars from these piles. As a general thing, as there is no yard at this place, the cars cannot be arranged according to the freight; consequently a good deal of labor and trucking is required to get it into the car. The freight for some firms in the West who have large daily shipments is put together at a certain place, and a car always left there, and, in general, great care is used to prevent long trucking. The handling of west-bound freight takes about 200 square feet to a car.

The method of loading and tallying is much the same as at Sixtieth street.

It may be well to note here that though a box can hold ten tons of miscellaneous merchandise, the average load is about six tons, as many stations require only part of a car-load as a general thing. This may be partly avoided by transfer stations at distributing points, but the work of transferring necessarily takes time, and, as promptness is one great element in railroad work, the establishment of these transfer stations is regulated more by the demands of business and competition than by the cost of operating. A long haul to a distributing point and short hauls beyond it may be favorable, or a comparatively short haul to a very large distributing point with many distinct long hauls beyond it. These transfer stations may be made to increase the average load of cars, and also their regularity in running, and it is probable that they are constantly attracting more attention from railroad managers.

The average total force employed at this station is : In the office, 30 clerks, messengers, etc.; and in the house, 300 laborers, tallymen, scalesmen, etc. The laborers are paid 17 cents an hour, and are worked only as needed. The average daily time at this station is about 12 hours.

On west-bound freight business, in busy seasons, the average work is 75 cars on Platform No. 1, 45 on No. 2, and 20 on No. 3.

On east-bound business it is about 45 cars a day on each of the Platforms No. 4, No. 5 and No. 6.

IN BROOKLYN, the Williamsburgh station is simply a covered pier for east-bound freight, on which the wagons drive and unload directly on the barge.

Refined sugar in barrels is the principal freight. One agent and about ten men are employed here.

LIGHTERAGE.—The lighterage equipment is as follows :

10 tugs for towing.

2 propellers carrying freight for quick delivery and having steam-hoisting machines.

33 barges, two of which have steam-hoisting machines.

40 canal boats for grain lighterage.

7 car floats.

This fleet is largely increased in busy times. It is managed by a private company.

TERMINAL WORK IN GENERAL.—It will be seen that this work, employing daily 1,300 men, 30 engines of all kinds, and 92 vessels, and using 110 tons of coal for handling 1,200 cars of freight a day, is carried on throughout with promptness and with the greatest attention to details.

If it is not perfect in its methods, it is more the fault of general arrangement than anything else, and it would seem that if any further improvement were possible in the work, it can only come from the further concentration of certain kinds of business and classes of work.

This can best be done permanently and effectually from full and accurate information and with the hearty co-operation of the merchants.

The following is a separation of expenses estimated from the annual report of this railroad company for the year 1883 :

Class of Expenses.	Freight Expenses chargeable to		
	Road work.	Station work.	Total.
Operating.			
Office	$24,688	$25,000	$49,688
Agents	22,398	940,000	962,398
Labor at stations		1,515,982	1,515,982
Switchmen	393,509	100,000	493,509
Fuel at water stations	31,293	10,000	41,293
Conductors, etc	480,361	100,000	580,361
Enginemen, etc	805,863	100,000	905,863
Fuel	1,329,617	200,000	1,529,617
Oil	136,706	30,000	166,706
Loss and damage	236,853	27,000	263,853
Salaries	94,705	20,000	114,705
Lighterage, rents, etc	62,904	900,000	962,904
Hire of cars	456,465	50,000	1,506,465
	$5,075,362	$4,017,982	$9,093,344

	Freight Expenses chargeable to		
Class of Expenses.	Road work.	Station work.	Total.
Brought forward.........	$5,075,362	$4,017,982	$9,093,344
Maintenance of road.			
Road bed.................	1,497,609	166,400	1,664,009
Fences...................	20,050	2,000	22,050
Rails.....................	493,190	8,000	501,190
Repairs to buildings.....	45,812	200,000	245,812
Taxes.....................	535,763	110,000	645,763
	2,592,424	486,400	3,078,824
Maintenance of cars			
Repairs of engines.......	636,368	120,000	756,368
Repairs of cars..........	1,727,630	300,000	2,027,630
Repairs of tools, etc....	68,366	7,000	75,366
Incidentals..............	126,003	14,000	140,003
	2,558,367	441,000	2,999,367
Total..............	$10,226,153	$4,945,382	$15,171,535

The total ton-mileage was 2,200,896,700, which gives an average cost of road work of 0.46 cent per ton-mile. The number of train-miles was about 11,000,000, or 92 cents per train-mile.

The number of tons hauled was 10,392,440, or about 45 cents for station work per ton *hauled*. But as the tons hauled were not all handled (some going to and from Boston and other places), it is likely, especially on account of the very heavy necessary expenses at New York, that the average cost of handling merchandise freight at this port is fully 60 cents per ton, the average cost of labor alone on this freight being about 30 cents per ton.

The cost of hauling on the Hudson River Division would be, according to the average rate (say 150 miles multiplied by 0.46 cent per mile), equal to 69 cents per ton, and it is quite likely, for various reasons, that it is not actually more than 65 cents on the Hudson River Division.

Hence it costs nearly as much per ton to handle freight at New York as it does to haul it between Albany and New York.

In regard to the time occupied in the terminal movement of freight, it is probable that the average time consumed in this work is nine hours on west-bound freight, from the time it is received at the freight station to its departure on the road

As regards the amount of room necessary in freight houses, the information given in this single description would seem to indicate that at lighterage stations west-bound freight promptly handled, weighed and sorted, requires the same amount of room in the freight houses as in the car ; and for east-bound freight, with longer temporary storage, six times the amount of room in the freight house that it does in the car. At city stations, west-bound freight promptly handled requires about three-quarters of the room in the freight house that it does in the car, and the east-bound freight about twice as much room.

Terminal Works and Business of the Pennsylvania Railroad.

The freight business of this road is divided into *main-line freight* on the Pennsylvania Railroad proper (New York to Pittsburgh and branch lines), *Western freight* on lines which it controls north and west of Pittsburg and Erie—this business is managed by the Union, Empire and Anchor fast freight lines—*Southern freight*, on the lines which it controls south of Philadelphia, and *Eastern freight*, between New England and points on the Pennsylvania Railroad system generally. For this latter business New York is a transfer and not a terminal station.

The Pennsylvania Railroad connects with and operates several distinct lines in the vicinity of New York, and as the only means of communication with the city is by water transportation from the New Jersey shore, the terminal freight stations and yards of this railroad system are numerous and widely scattered. They are:

In New Jersey: First, the terminal yard and shops at the Meadows. Second, the through Western freight station and transfers, the grain elevators and the stock yards and abattoir, all at Harsimus Cove, Jersey City. Third, the main line freight station and transfer and the Red Star and Netherlands steamship docks, adjoining the passenger station, at Jersey city. Fourth, the oil yard at Communipaw. Fifth, the coal docks of the Amboy Division at South Amboy.

In New York City: At five separate localities on the Hudson River docks are six freight stations, used for the local freight business of the city.

In Brooklyn: At Williamsburgh is a freight dock used largely for the shipment of sugar from the Brooklyn refineries.

On the Harlem River there is a transfer for Eastern freight, and also one *on the Hudson River* at Fishkill. Neither of these is operated by this company.

TERMINAL YARDS AT THE MEADOWS.—The first available site for a yard west of Bergen Hill is where the grade of the railroad descends to the level of the marshy land west of the Hackensack River (about four miles from the Hudson River), on the long and narrow strip lying between the main tracks of this railroad and the Delaware, Lackawanna & Western Railroad.

The construction was begun about 1872, and the yard was first used in 1874. The site, formerly under water, had been reclaimed by a dike. The surface was properly ditched, cribs sunk where necessary, and gravel brought in by train. The bank being very light, there was little disturbance of the original surface. The general plan consists of eight tracks, parallel to the main tracks forming four yards by means of lines of cross-overs located about ¼ mile apart. The three-throw switches are made of two No. 8 rail frogs and one No. 10, with upright stands; they work well. The grades, following the surface of ground, are light, and neither materially help nor retard the work of drilling. There are about 19 miles of available track in the sidings.

Operation: The engine from the incoming train from the West is detached at the west end of the yard, and the yard engine on the adjacent track, by means of a pushing pole, cuts the train up; this is done according to destination, and in a general way, as to classes of freight. Fast through freight is placed on the section of tracks called "Merchandise Yard;" slow through and local on "Coal Yard," etc. The yard engine then pulls them out on the northerly track to the different Jersey City yards, bringing back empty cars, which are placed on the tracks for empty cars. This work generally requires, night and day, four engines in the yard and two running to Jersey City. With this equipment, in the year 1883 there were received 214,863 loaded cars of all kinds from the West, and 151,592 were forwarded west from Jersey City and from this yard.

The following is the organization at this yard. It applies generally to all yards, except that it varies in the numbers according to the size of the yard and the work done:

	Day.	Night.
Yard-Master	1	1
Assistant Yard-Master, east-bound freight	1	1
" " west-bound freight	2	2
" " local freight	3	0
Yard clerks	4	2
Car record clerks	2	2
Lock and seal clerks	2	2
Weigh clerks	1	0
Coal clerks	1	0
Watchmen	2	2
Switchmen		

Each of the six engines have the following crew, night and day: 1 engineer, 1 fireman, 1 conductor, 1 flagman and 2 brakemen.

HARSIMUS COVE TERMINUS—JERSEY CITY.— This (Plate A) is on the Hudson River, about 1,200 ft. north of the Jersey City passenger and freight yard. It has a double-track

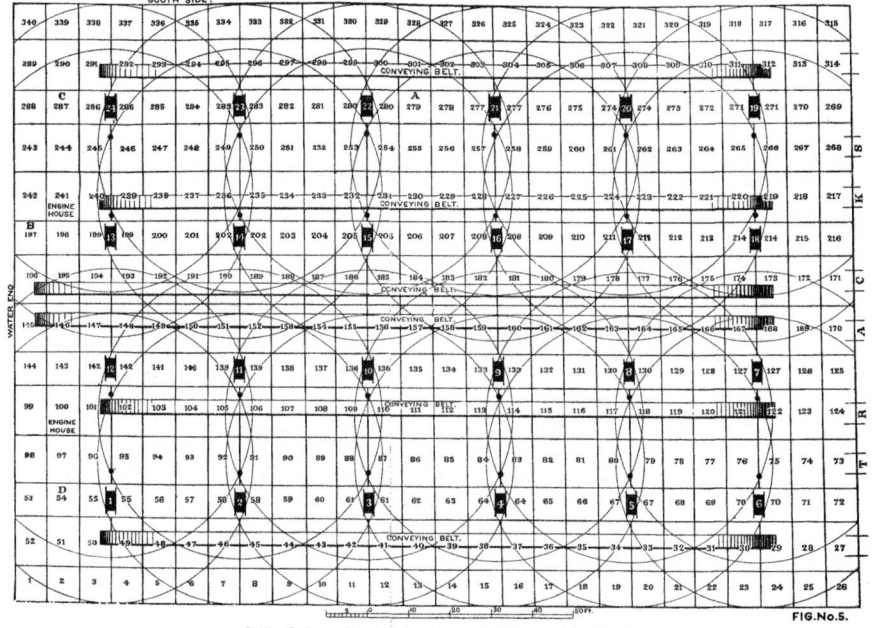

PLAN OF GRAIN ELEVATOR AT HARSIMUS COVE, JERSEY CITY, N. J.   FIG. No. 5.

connection with the main line, about one mile long, built on trestle-work, crossing the city streets above grade. The elevator, instead of being on its own pier, is located inland between the piers, with its end only toward the water, on account of the scarcity of water front controlled by the company, and also to enable ocean steamers to lie along the pier and receive grain by the conveyers and merchandise from the freight pier at the same time. There was also a rock foundation at its present site.

The tracks were formerly built on trestle-work, but when the new work was done in 1880 they were filled in with street refuse from New York, top-dressed with ashes. This material was cheap and light in weight, causing little disturbance of the silt lying on the rock bottom, which dips rapidly toward the river. The tracks keep in excellent shape, are laid of new material, and are generally 11 ft. between centres. The switches are almost entirely single-throw, split switches, with steel coil springs; the frogs are No. 8 and No. 6 rail. There are 14 miles of track in the yard.

The construction of the piers and freight houses is indicated on Plate B. The sides are corrugated iron; the roof, gravel; the piles are not driven to the rock; they are about 80 ft. long, and are not spliced, nor pointed, but driven with a square end down. The freight houses are neatly whitewashed inside and kept very neat. The following are some of the particulars of the size and cost of these sheds:

```
Floor area of New Shed Pier No. 2 (see fig. 3):           Sq. ft.
   First floor, North platform..........................  32,000
   First floor, South    "    west-bound...............  11,000
                                                          ------
      Total....................................           43,000
   Second floor, North platform.........................  31,000
                South    "    ........................    9,000
                                                          ------
      Floor area, total..................................  40,000
   Old Shed, North platform.............................  54,000
             South   "    ...........................    16,000
                                                          ------
      Floor area, total.................................  70,000
Pier No. 3 Shed (see fig. 4):
   8 ft. centre to centre of pile bents.
   16 "     "       "     "  house sections.
   32 "     "       "     "  side doors.
   7 ft. x 8 ft., size of upper doors.
   11 ft. x 12 ft., size of lower doors.
   Area, 2 lower platforms, each 35,000 sq. ft...........  70,000
         2 upper     "      "    30,000   "  ..........   60,000
                                                          -------
                                                          130,000
```
Cost of shed, about 90 cents per sq. ft. of total area of lower floor.
Cost of pier, about 100 cents per sq. ft.

The grain elevator, the plan of which is shown by fig. 5, was built in 1879–80, and is constructed of heavy timber framework, founded on rock from 12 to 26 ft. below the surface. The foundation of each post is a separate pier, the coffer dams used in the construction generally inclosed four piers. The boxes or legs in which the elevators work are of boiler iron, and are shown in black with white figures in the plan; the weighing bins and spouts are of iron; the sheathing of the sides of the building is corrugated iron. Those parts of the framework lying under compression are oak. The engines are situated on the bin floor, 90 ft. above the ground; they consist of two pair of double engines, making in all four cylinders, 20 × 24, running four 48 in. driving belts, and are of 100 horse-power each. The weighing bins are in pairs, two to each scale; the capacity of each bin is 36,000 lbs. Each was intended when the elevator was built to hold a car-load, enabling the scales to be kept constantly at work. The contract price of the building was $450,000.

Operation of the Yard: The yard engines at Harsimus Cove receive the trains from the Meadows engine and sort them more thoroughly on the tracks marked K. Freight from and to transfer bridges are put on W and E respectively; for the elevator on G and empty cars from the elevator on F; Piers 1 and 2 freight on P. The part marked R is the freight yard under the charge of the local agent. (The freight is here delivered directly to the city drays.) West-bound freight is hauled directly from this yard, and does not stop at the Meadows. The track scales are at S, the water stand-pipe at C. Five switch engines are employed, two constantly at the transfer bridges work; the pier freight houses generally require two and sometimes three shifts a day. The general grade of the yard falls slightly toward the river, and, especially at the head of the yard, materially aids the work of drilling.

Operation of the Elevator: Before the cars loaded with grain enter the elevator, the agent of the Produce Exchange inspects and "grades" each car-load; this is done in the yard. The cars are then run into the house and the contents elevated, weighed and run into the bins, where the grain is stored according to grade and not according to owners. The business of the elevator, as is usual, consists of handling the grain, storage and cleaning. The cleaning (only when requested by the owners) is done by blowing a stream of air through the grain after it leaves the weighing bins. It is then elevated again and again weighed, the dirt falling to the ground floor. The charge for this work is one quarter of a cent a bushel. A regular charge is also made for storage of certain kinds of grain after a period agreed upon, generally ten days. The weighing and general methods are those usually employed in receiving and delivering grain in elevators, except that as the grain is delivered by belt conveyers, the bins are all operated alike, none being exclusively devoted to shipping nor to transfer. They all receive and all deliver, and the transfer from one bin to another is made by spout, or when necessary by belt. These endless belt conveyers run horizontally from end to end of building on the bin floors; they are made of rubber, are 36 in. wide, and each one of the six in use can carry 8,000 to 10,000 bushels an hour. Grain is lifted from the bins, runs through an adjustable sheet-iron spout, and falls on the top or carrying portion of the endless belt, which runs at a rapid rate toward the river, and at the return of the belt the grain (which is spread on the belt in a layer about 3 in. deep) shoots forward and runs down the sheet-iron spouts extending from the shore-end of the building. Three of these spouts lead to the bulkhead, where there is sufficient dock room for small boats— such as canal boats—which are used as grain lighters. Six spouts lead to the long gallery belts, the position of which is shown in the plan and section of the freight sheds. These gallery belts convey the grain to large boats lying along the piers. For the purpose of delivering the grain at several points along the pier, the upper or carrying part of the belt is raised, at any point desired, by a loose roller mounted on a movable iron frame about 4 ft. high, and as the belt falls by its own weight away from the roller, the grain shoots ahead in the upward direction in which it was traveling, and falls into a box made with one spout on the side and one in front, over the belt.

In the box is a movable partition which separates the grain in any desired proportion, one portion falling through the side spout into the sheet-iron tubes, which carry it to the vessel, and the remainder falls through the front spout upon the belt and is carried along by it to another delivery spout. These belts are operated by independent 30 horse-power engines working at the shore end of the galleries.

It requires 20 tons of coal a day to operate the entire elevator, working at an average rate, and 13 tons when work is slack. The capacity for receiving and delivering grain in this elevator with 24 legs and 6 belts is very great; indeed, the size of the yard and the movement of cars is more a measure of its work than its own capacity. A good average of continuous work has been 100 cars a day, though over 200 cars are sometimes unloaded in one day, and 156 cars were lately unloaded here in the forenoon with six gangs of shovelers unloading the cars ; but the rapidity of the work somewhat depends on the character and condition of the grain. The storage capacity is about 1,500,000 bushels : 9,000,000 bushels of grain were delivered by this railroad in 1883.

Organization : The working organization of the elevator is as follows :

1 Superintendent and clerks ;

1 General Foreman over all workmen, and with him 1 car record clerk and 1 shipping clerk ;

1 Master Machinist, who has special charge of keeping all machinery in repair, and under him 2 assistants on repair work and 3 oilers ;

1 Wharf-master, who provides boats and directs their loading, and who has charge of the trimmers ;

On the Track Floor : 1 Foreman of shovelers, and under him 12 laborers at the shovels and 2 opening cars ;

On the Bin Floor : 1 Foreman and 2 men setting spouts, etc., under general direction of the weighman on the floor above ; 1 engineer-in-chief, who runs one main engine and has oversight of the engineers who run the other engines ; also over the firemen, of whom there are 2 during the day and 1 at night ;

On the Scale Floor : 1 Chief Weighman, who weighs all grain coming into the house and directs its distribution ; 2 assistant weighmen, who weigh the grain shipped from the house ;

In the Galleries : 1 Foreman, with 3 men, who attend to the loading and unloading of the delivery belt, and 1 man to attend to the three small engines which run the gallery belts.

Operations of the Piers in General : The piers at this place are almost entirely used for the lighterage business of through Western freight, moved in car-load lots ; of freight coming from the West— flour for instance—to be lightered to a ship for foreign export, or to storage warehouses located on the water; and of freight going to the West—sugar for instance—lightered (or transferred directly) from ships, or from manufactories and warehouses ; in this way saving the hauling to the railroad freight stations in New York. This through business is under the management of the fast-freight lines, which are organizations of agencies managing that portion of the western business of this railroad system which extends over lines connected with, or controlled by, but not operated by, the Pennsylvania Railroad proper.

All transfers to or from large ships are done at these piers, whether on main line or Western business ; hence, although for the sake of proper operation the business at Harsimus Cove is mostly confined to fast-freight line business, it is not exclusively, nor is the loading entirely, done in fast-freight line cars, though considerable effort is made to do so. This is desirable in order to keep cars running in certain beats, one class for long and one class for short hauls; for in railroad management constant effort is made to attain in all things a systematic operation of business, classified in character and concentrated in location, and just how far this can be profitably done is a subject of constant thought and experiment.

Except the hydraulic elevators hereafter mentioned, there is no stationary machinery for loading, unloading or moving freight on any of these piers; the only machine for moving it is the hand truck. Two lighters, used for freight requiring quick delivery, have both steam-hoisting and propelling apparatus; a few have steam hoists and are moved by separate propellers, but most of them have only the gaff boom and hand drum. These are operated either by hand or by an independent boat carrying a steam hoist especially for this purpose, or by one on an idle lighter alongside.

The unloading of ships and independent lighters is done by city stevedores, and not by the railroad company.

The approximate daily work at the freight houses on these piers is 145 loaded cars of east-bound freight and 50 cars of west-bound, requiring about 225 truckmen and tallymen for handling the freight.

Operation of Pier No. 1: This is not covered, and is used for the direct transfer of such freight as building material, machinery and iron manufactures which do not require storage, inspection, or piece-weighing, but are directly transferred by lighters to destination. There is no platform, and the cars are seldom loaded here with west-bound freight.

Operation of Pier No. 2: In the old freight house, marked *D*, "wet" freight, such as bacon, sugar in hogsheads, and cotton, copper matte and other merchandise in car-load lots requiring weighing, inspection or temporary storage, is handled to and from the cars. In this house the weighing is done on movable scales. The wide platform between the water and the track is mostly used; the other platform is out of the way for lighterage business and more convenient for transfer to cars on the track on the south side. The new shed, marked *A*, has two stories, and is mostly used as an export flour depot. On the wide platform were three *hydraulic* elevators, 8 ft. × 8 ft., capable of lifting 22 barrels, but generally lifting 16. They worked excellently in summer, but the water froze in the pipes under the wharf in winter, and steam power has been substituted. The narrow or south platform is used for general transfer from lighters of merchandise moving west, such as imported wire or sugar from the refineries, the only difference in operation being that local freight must give way to fast through freight. There are three stationary platform scales on this platform, as shown on the plan ; they are placed between the doors.

Operation of Pier No. 3 : This house is devoted to dry freight, such as flour, oil-cake, machinery and boxed groceries. The second floor has not yet been used. The uncovered portion of the end of the pier is used for transfer between ships and cars of certain freight, as imported lumber, which may be left exposed if the transfer cannot be made at once. About 1,430,000 barrels of flour were delivered by this railroad in 1883.

Operation of the Transfer Bridges : Freight shipped eastward for use or sale in New York and westward from New York merchants in car-load lots, or less, is not lightered across the river as it was before 1866. The cars themselves are now carried across on barges or floats, which generally have two lines of track and hold ten cars, five on a side, with a raised platform between the tracks. The transfer bridges carrying the tracks, by means of which the cars are run on and off these floats, are Howe truss bridges, 100 ft. long, hinged at the shore end and suspended by heavy iron chains from a stationary frame-work near the river end. They are thus, by means of the chains, which run over large sheave wheels above, and are worked by hand gear below, made adjustable to the stage of the tide and the load on the float. These bridges are located at *A* and *B* on the plan. The through New England freight is also transferred over these bridges to three track floats, holding 14 cars, and having no platform in the centre. This business amounts to about 150 cars a day. Coal for New England is also transferred over these bridges to large floats holding 20 cars, which are towed to Fishkill-on-the-Hudson, about 60 miles up the river.

JERSEY CITY TERMINUS.—This (Plate A) adjoins the passenger station on the north. It is the original yard, where the whole business was formerly moved. It is short and wide, and has been developed, or spread out like a fan, from the narrow entrance at the head. At the busiest point in the yard there is a dangerous crossing of a city street, which is guarded by six men with flags.

The track is furnished mostly with three-throw switches. There are five miles of available shifting tracks in the freight yard.

The sheds on the piers are ordinary one-story wooden sheds, with a wooden truss roof. The sheds are covered with corrugated iron on the outside, and are neatly whitewashed on the inside.

The transfer house, marked T, is an ordinary temporary shed inserted on the only spare room in the yard. It is built between the tracks without a platform on the outside, and hence the cars frequently require shifting, so as to make the car-door correspond with the door of the house. This would not be necessary if there was a platform on the outside, or if the house covered the tracks as well as the platform between them.

Operation of the Yard: There are four engines in use here, night and day, one of them constantly on the transfer bridge work. Each engine has one day's rest for cleaning in the week, only two working on Sunday. The cars which go to the docks of the Red Star and Netherlands lines of steamers are hauled by horses. West-bound freight from the transfer bridges is placed on tracks marked W; east-bound on tracks marked E.

Operation of the Piers in General: This is similar to that at Harsimus Cove, and is devoted to the lighterage business of car-load lots of main line and Southern freight. The west-bound freight lightered from ships, storehouses and factories is much heavier than, sometimes twice, the east-bound freight; hence a separate house is devoted to it. A small quantity of through Western freight is moved at these docks, as there is a derrick here (L on plan) of large capacity, and there is nothing of the kind at Harsimus Cove. There is no steam or hydraulic machinery used here; but there are some small hand derricks on the north side of Pier E. The freight is moved in the house by ordinary hand trucks, excepting hogsheads of imported sugar weighing 2,000 lbs. and over, which are moved by special iron-frame trucks, by means of which three men can truck them instead of rolling them. Also in the New England transfer house, where a great variety of merchandise is handled, there is an ordinary four-wheel truck without a handle, about 8 in. square and having wheels 4 in. in diameter, which is found very useful for moving boxes, either too heavy or too bulky for the ordinary hand truck. At these piers can be seen the loading of what is called the "fast local freight" on the Pennsylvania Railroad. This is a service induced by the competition of the Philadelphia & Reading system west of Lancaster. The packages are very carefully loaded in the cars, the first to go in being the last to come out. The train is run on fast time, and by having a few additional train hands, the delivery is quickly made.

The daily work here is about 90 cars west-bound and 60 cars east-bound, with 125 laborers, etc., and about 50 cars at the New England transfer, with 18 laborers.

Operation of Pier E: This is used for the transfer of west-bound freight from lighters. Freight is hoisted from the lighters and trucked and piled on the platform, or trucked directly into the cars. There is not much storage required here, and a large part of the shed is devoted to track room, three tracks running the whole length of the building, as shown on the plan. Area of platform is 8,000 square feet.

Operation of Pier D: This is used for the transfer of east-bound freight to the lighters. The northern part is uncovered and the transfer is made direct, as at Pier No. 1, Harsimus Cove. The southern portion is covered and is used for temporary storage and inspection. By a rule of the Produce Exchange, the railroad companies are obliged to give five days' storage to flour for inspection, and therefore much space is devoted to this at all the docks where flour is handled. Area of platform is 19,000 square feet.

Operation of Transfer House : The cars are loaded on the New England roads with freight mixed as to destination on the Pennsylvania Railroad system. These cars are placed on each side of the transfer sheds at this place ; the freight is then taken out and sorted on the platform according to destination, and reloaded in the same cars. It is simply a sorting process of the freight, and is not intended to regulate the car service any more than that the cars are reloaded so as to go as near home as possible. There are similar transfers at Mantua, where the main line and Southern freight divide, and at Pittsburgh for the different Western lines.

Operation of Transfer Bridges: This is exactly similar to that at Harsimus Cove. Eastern freight transfer is done mostly by 'a side-wheel steamer having two tracks, each holding seven cars. Both passenger and freight trains are transferred on this boat. It makes four trips a day with freight. The largest work done over these bridges is transferring cars to the floats for the New York docks—about 150 cars every day.

NEW YORK CITY FREIGHT DOCKS.—The Pennsylvania Railroad freight docks, as the accompaning plan shows, are altogether on the west side of New York, on the Hudson River. As shown, most of them face on West street, which is at present of very irregular width. A general plan has been adopted by the Department of Docks of the city for the improvement of this water front, and is prosecuted by that department with as much

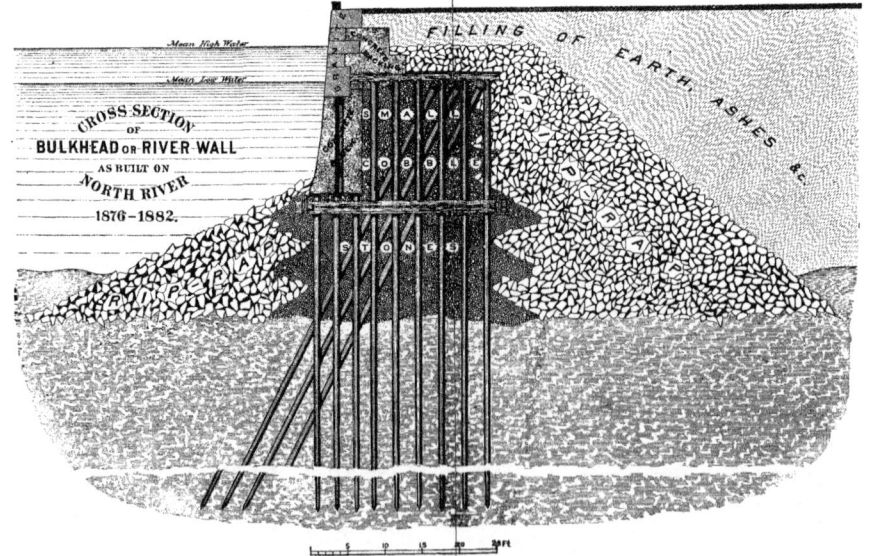

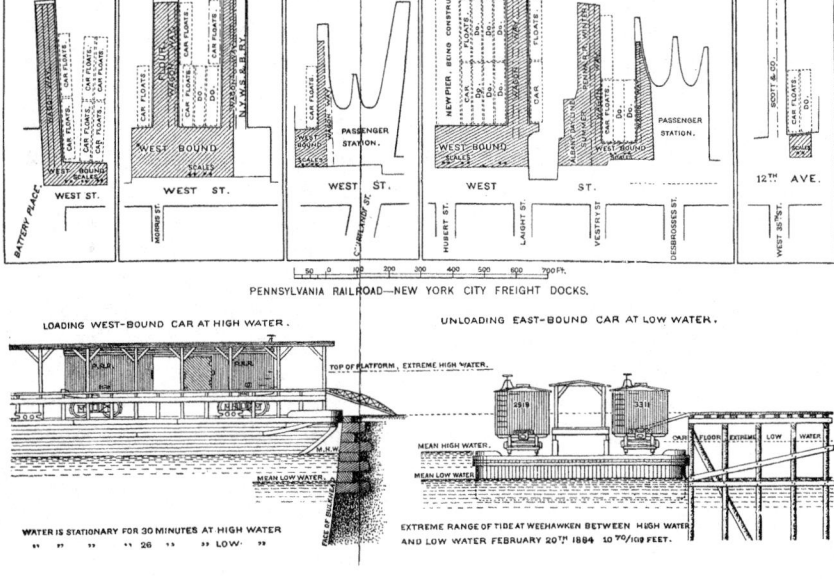

PENNSYLVANIA RAILROAD—NEW YORK CITY FREIGHT DOCKS.

energy as circumstances permit; and a great improvement has been made within the last ten years. The plan calls for a width of 250 ft. from the east building line of West street to the bulkhead wall, and from this wall piers ranging from 75 to 100 ft. in width extend into the water. It would seem to be impossible to make any decided improvement in the general methods of moving freight in the city before the docks are permanently arranged and constructed, and West street opened throughout as designed.

The general arrangement of all the railroad freight docks is the same, but there is no standard, and the unsettled condition of the docks causes many changes in details of construction. The construction of the bulkhead wall is shown in the accompanying plan. The method of construction is as follows: The mud and silt are dredged out to a depth of about 35 ft. below low water; 8 ft. of gravel is then thrown in and protected by riprap thrown on the sides, as is shown. The piles are then driven, and more gravel and riprap thrown between them. Those piles which hold the concrete blocks are sawed off level by a circular saw rigged on a scow. A top dressing of fine gravel is then spread, and a "poultice" of cement mortar in gunny baga is then placed on top of each pile, and the concrete block is placed in position by a 100-ton floating derrick, constructed for this service. From this bulkhead wall juts the pier.

Piles can be got 90 ft. long, and even when they are very easily driven, the friction is ample after the settlement of the silt around them.

The concrete blocks are 12 ft. in length longitudinally, are made of one part cement, two parts sand, and five parts broken stone. Each block weighs from 70 to 74 tons.

A pier 75 ft wide, such as was lately constructed on Pier No. 27, has 14 piles (5 ft. 10 in. from centre to centre) in each bent, with a brace pile at one end. The first span from the bulkhead is about 16 ft., then 9 ft., spans to within five bents of the end, where the bents are 12½ ft. between the centres. On account of running ice and the exposed position of these outside bents, they are constructed of columns of squared timber 10 in. × 10 in., bolted together, making a cross section 20 in. × 20 in., shod with an iron shoe, and driven by a 6,000-lb hammer with a 12 ft. fall. They are protected with an iron casing above low water. The bents are capped across the pier and longitudinal stringers, 12 in. × 12 in., drift-bolted on top of the caps, 5 ft. 10 in. between centres. Across the stringers are spiked 4-in. creosoted plank, laid 10 in. apart and 3 in. plank spiked over these, laid close together diagonally. A heavy fender is bolted to the piles along the slip. The contract price for removing the old pier and building the new pier, No. 27 (shown on fig. 7) was $40,000. These piers are covered with a one story warehouse built by the railroad company.

The bulkhead is covered with a frame shed, with offices on the second floor.

Operation: There are no transfer bridges down-town on this side of the river at present in operation by this company, and the general method of handling the freight is by hand-trucking to and from the cars on the floats. On most of the piers are hand derricks for moving heavy freight, but there is no other machinery of any kind, either steam or hydraulic.

The following list gives the general character of business:

Main Line and Southern Freight: Pier 1.—Any quantity of Pennsylvania Railroad and Southern freight, and car-loads from Kensington, Pennsylvania.

Pier 16.—Any quantity of New York Division freight and of south-bound Baltimore freight.

Pier 39.—Any quantity of Philadelphia and Pennsylvania Railroad Division and Southern freight, and car loads only of United New Jersey Division freight.

Freight to All Destinations: Foot of Thirty-fifth Street.—Any quantity of main line Southern and Western freight, and car-loads only of lake freight.

Western Freight: Piers 4 and 5.—Any quantity of Western freight, and car-loads only of certain stations on the Philadelphia & Erie.

Piers 27 and 28.—Any quantity of Western freight and car-loads only of lake freight.

Approximate work for one day (probably more than the average):

No. of Pier.	Loaded Cars, East-bound.	Cars, West-bound.	No. of Truckmen, Weighmen, etc.
1	70	50	80
4 and 5	75	50	90
16	40	40	40
27 and 28	50	75	90
39	50	90	125
35th street	10	30	25
Total	295	235	450
Percentage	47	53	..

The general method of handling freight is as follows: East-bound freight is trucked from the cars on the float to the pier, and is sorted according to consignees to some extent and piled for temporary storage. The city drays enter from the street and drive along the track marked " wagon way" on the plan, which is simply a part of the pier on which no freight is piled, but on the same level as the rest of the pier, except at Pier 16, where the wagon way is separated from the freight shed, and is on a slightly lower level. The freight is loaded on the drays by outside laborers hired by the draymen and paid generally by the piece. The admission of these wagons on the dock often causes a blockade and inconvenience of work to the railroad men handling the freight. As the sheds are all one-story, this wagon way, as is shown on the plan, occupies approximately 21½ per cent. of the total effective area (considering it as a freight house with a track on the outside), and consequently 21½ per cent. of the annual rental is devoted to this purpose. It is thus found necessary to spend, say, $2,000 a month for what would be considered under any other circumstances a very awkward, inefficient arrangement, being simply a series of blind alleys, ranging from 14 ft. to 16 ft. in width and from 500 to 600 ft. in length. The estimate of area shows, what is very evident by observation, that a wide pier and a deep shed on the bulkhead form the most economical arrangement, giving the greatest relative area for storage, and hence the least relative area for the simple operations of handling freight. This is evident by comparing Piers 4 and 5 with either Pier 1 or Pier 39. The east-bound freight is delivered at all times during the day up to six o'clock. There is no charge made for storage, but if goods remain for some time un-called for they are sent to some private storehouse.

West-bound freight is unloaded from the city drays into the bulkhead shed, weighed and sorted according to destination if it is not directly loaded upon the cars. The scales are placed in pairs, as shown on the plan. After being sorted and piled, the freight is moved on hand trucks from the bulkhead, along the platform on the float, into the cars. The average haul of the hand trucks is, say, 140 ft. at Piers 4 and 5, and 240 ft. at Piers 27 and 28. The rise and fall of the tide changes the position of the level of the platform, and, as is shown, often requires a heavy lift at a considerable expense of labor. The west-bound freight is received up to 4 P. M. This rule was adopted in order to enable the freight to be shipped promptly each night, and to induce the shippers to forward it during the fore part of the day.

It may be well to note here one instance of the money value of promptness and system in work. As shown by the approximate estimate, 53 per cent. of the number of cars, and probably 50 per cent. of the number of tons, is west-bound freight, and this is handled in 24 per cent. of the total area, and, consequently, only 24 per cent. of the annual rental, considering it as a freight house, is applied to this movement.

The wages of the truckmen are 17 cents an hour. They generally work 12 hours in the day, as they are often kept loading until 8 p. m. One gang generally loads one car every half hour. The cars are always carefully loaded, so that the first freight to come out is the last to go in.

The general organization of the freight stations on this road is similar to the one which we give below, which applies to a freight station on the New York docks : 1 agent and clerks ; 1 superintendent of freight house and 1 clerk.

On West-bound Freight: 1 weigh-master to each scale ; 1 scale clerk to each pair of scales, who records the number and weight of each package ; 1 receiving clerk to each pair of scales, who signs the shipping bill, compares and checks it and the duplicate, which is sent to the agent's office. The scale clerk and receiving clerk make entirely separate records, and thus form a check on each other. The freight is sorted and piled according to destination by "switchmen," or by ordinary truckmen under the superintendent's directions. Each gang loading the freight consists of nine men, two stevedores, who pack the freight in the cars ; five truckmen, who truck the freight ; one loader, who loads the trucks ; one tallyman, who is stationed at the car and records in a book the number of the car, the names of the stevedores, the date, the time of beginning and ending of the loading of each car, and the consignee, number, weight and contents of each piece. At the fast freight stations, as soon as a car is loaded, the tallyman sends his book to the agent's office, and the pieces are checked with the duplicate shipping bills and the car manifests are made out, and on them the number of the tallyman's book is put.

On East-bound Freight.—The same gangs are used to unload as to load. The tallyman here also keeps a separate account of each piece on a sheet arranged for the purpose, and sends the sheet to the agent's office as soon as the car is unloaded, where it is compared with the manifests. The delivery clerks, who are stationed at the gate, copy each consignee's bill in a book, and the city drayman receipts in the book, which can be compared with the tallyman's sheets and manifests. It is seen that in this whole system there is a complete series of checks for each man's work, and he is made to feel responsible for it. The system also enables goods to be easily traced.

The force at *every* freight station is organized into a fire brigade and regularly drilled. Posters are in each building giving the duties and station of each man and the signals ; and electric alarm signals are numerous.

LIGHTERAGE.—The effective freight lighterage equipment of this company, according to the report of 1883, is :

1 freight steamboat on " Eastern" freight.
14 tugs. Cost about $25,000 each.
48 car floats (carrying 8 and 10 cars). Cost $13,000 each.
2 steam lighters.
17 lighters.
15 barges.
8 canal boats.

TERMINAL WORK IN GENERAL: From the report of the Pennsylvania Railroad Company for 1883, the following statistics are obtained of the freight business of the United Railroads in New Jersey Division, between all the New Jersey railroads operated by the Pennsylvania Railroad Company :

Total freight ton-mileage, 1883, 542,827,918.
Average cost of transporting each ton of freight one mile, 1.167 cents.
Total expenses.

Conducting transportation	$3,596,927.80
Motive-power	1,489,446.06
Maintenace of way	905,783.49
Maintenance of cars	307,152.92
General expenses	33,499.27
Total	$6,332,809.54

The following separation is copied or deduced from the report, and is given as an approximation :

	Hauling.	Handling.	Total.
Conducting transportation, conductors and brakemen	$442,598.30	$50,000.00	$492,598.30
Dispatchers, telegraph, etc	357,120.11		357,120.11
Car service	303,483.99		303,483.99
Labor at stations		672,594.54	672,594.54
Agents and clerks		475,750.80	475,750.80
Lighterage, docks, etc.		1,295,380.06	1,295,380.06
Total	$1,103,202.40	$2,493,725.40	$3,596,927.80
Motive power	1,234,241.84	255,204.22	1,489,446.06
Maintenance of way.	805,783.49	100,000.00	905,783.49
Maintenance of cars.	344,152.92	63,000.00	307,152.92
Total	$3,387,380.65	$2,911,929.62	$6,299,310.27
General expenses			33,499.27
Total			$6,332,809.54

This statement shows that, considering the New Jersey railroads as a whole, the work at stations and yards costs nearly as much as

SCHEDULE OF FREIGHT MOVEMENT AT NEW YORK TERMINI.

Movement.	Main Line and Southern Merchandise.	Western Merchandise.		Grain.	Oil.	Live Stock.	Coal.	
To and from following receiving stations on N. J. shore:	Jersey City Freight Docks.	Harsimus Cove.	Red Star and Netherlands Docks.	Harsimus Cove.	Communipaw.	Harsimus Cove.	South Amboy.	Harsimus Cove.
Moved by lighters to and from......	"Stores" and Vessels.	"Stores" and Vessels.	....	"Stores" and Vessels.	"Stores" and Vessels.	"Stores" and Vessels.	"Stores" and Vessels.	....
Moved by floats to and from.........	4 N. Y. freight Docks and New England R. R.	3 N. Y. freight Docks and New England R. R.	....	....	....	....	....	New England R. R.
Moved on hand trucks to and from	Vessels and Lighters.	Vessels and Lighters.	Vessels and Lighters.	....	....	....	....	....
Moved by gravity or machinery to..	....	....	....	Vessels and Lighters.	....	....	Vessels and Lighters.	....

This railroad does not deliver any great amount of hay or dairy products, but it brings large quantities of perishable fruit from the South.

the work on the road, and as the terminal work on the New York Division is much larger in proportion than the station and yard work on the other railroads of the system, it is likely that, taking this work as a whole, the cost of moving a ton of freight between the Meadows yard and the New York city drays is greater than that between the Meadows yard and Philadelphia. It may be possible that this terminal work will hereafter be more completely arranged and concentrated, and that by the introduction of some simple form of steam machinery for hauling freight longitudinally in the house this work can be done more cheaply than it is at present and quite as promptly.

The conditions to be observed are so various, however, that it is questionable if any mechanical method of moving either east or west-bound freight on these piers can be successfully applied, although it would seem worthy of study and experiment.

The following table is added for easy reference. It gives a comparison of the reports of the New York Central & Hudson River Railroad and the United Railroads of New Jersey Division of the Pennsylvania Railroad for 1883. These roads are double and four-tracked trunk-line railroads entering the port of New York. Each has numerous branches running through a populous country. They differ greatly in the length of line (as is shown) and also in the amount of coal carried, it being only one-fifth of the tonnage of the New York Central to about three-eighths on the United Railroads of New Jersey.

The difference in the proportion of the mileage of branches to main line lessens the value of this comparison, except as between the New Jersey system of the Pennsylvania Railroad and the New York system of the New York Central. The reports are given in such shape that a more just comparison cannot be made. A great deal of the information (as is shown) is derived from estimates and not taken from accurate data, hence it is not intended to be a critical comparison, but simply one which shows the differences in characteristics and business. The statistics of the work of handling would be better if they could be given per ton handled instead of per ton hauled :

	N. Y. Cen. & Hudson River.	United Railroads of N.J.
Fixtures :		
1. Miles of main line (c)	441.75	90.76
2. Miles of road, main line and branches (c)	993.29	435.07
3. Miles of track (c)	2,684.88	930.49
4. Miles of track per mile of road (d)	2.7	2.14
5. Number of city stations (e)	20	8
Earnings :		
6. Total freight earnings (c)	$21,133,766	$8,269,942

	N. Y. Cen. & Hudson River.	United Railroads of N.J.
7. Total freight expenses (c)	$15,171,535	$6,299,310
8. Net freight earnings (c)	5,967,231	1,970,632
9. Average total freight earnings per ton-mile (c)	0.91	1.47
10. Average total freight expenses per ton-mile (c)	0.68	1.17
11. Average net freight earnings per ton-mile (c)	0.23	0.30
Tonnage:		
12. Total tons hauled (c)	10,892,440	8,855,567
13. Total tons of through freight hauled (c)	1,813,320	2,611,000
14. Total tons of local freight hauled (c)	9,079,120	6,244,567
15. Per cent. of local freight to total tons hauled (d)	83	70
16. Average tonnage per mile of road (d)	2,215,764	1,247,684
17. Average tonnage per mile of track (d)	820,000	583,000
Mileage:		
18. Average mileage or "haul" per ton, miles (d)	202	61.3
19. Total ton-mileage (c)	2,200,896,780	542,829,918
20. Total ton-mileage of through freight (e)	725,328,000	234,995,000
21. Total ton-mileage of local freight (e)	1,475,568,780	307,834,918
Hauling—		
22. Total hauling expenses (e)	$10,226,142	$3,388,323
23. Per cent. of total expenses (e)	67½	54
24. Average hauling expenses per ton-mile (e)	0.46 ct.	0.62 ct.
25. Average hauling expenses per mile of road (e)	$10,290	$7,788
Handling—		
26. Total handling expenses (e)	4,945,382	2,910,986
27. Per cent. of total expenses (e)	32½	46
28. Average handling expenses per ton hauled (e)	$0.45	$0.33
29. Average tons hauled per city station	544,622	1,106,941
30. New York through freight—		
Cost of handling per ton (e)	$0.60	$0.60
Average cost of hauling (e)	2.02	0.53
Average total cost (e)	2.62	1.13
Average cost per ton-mile (e)	0.60	1.26
31. Local freight—		
Average cost of handling, all stations (e)	0.42	0.25
Average cost of hauling (e)	0.75	0.30
Average total cost (e)	1.17	0.55
Average length of haul, miles (e)	164	49
Average cost per ton-mile (e)	0.71 ct.	1.124 cts.

(c) signifies copied.
(d) " deducted.
(e) " estimated.

Remarks.—Line 4; the difference here is largely caused by the length of "turnouts" on the New York Central Division.

Line 9.—Water and other competition on the New York Central probably causes this difference.

Line 10.—The relatively large terminal expenses (at New York mostly) on the Pennsylvania causes this difference. See lines 22 and 26.

Line 20.—This is calculated on a basis of 400 miles average haul of through freight on the New York Central, taking into account the Boston freight leaving the road at Albany. This is only used to get the ton-mileage of local freight, line 21.

Line 16.—Shows the equivalent number of tons hauled once over the whole road (main line and branches), and shows that the New York system moves on an average nearly twice the number of tons of freight over every mile of road, and 1.4 the number of tons over every mile of track that the New Jersey system does. See line 17.

Line 25.—Shows the average cost of the work of hauling over a mile of road, and at 5 per cent. interest gives an average value of $205,800 per mile for the New York system and $155,760 per mile for the New Jersey system, taking the freight expenses alone as the guide.

Line 28.—This difference is caused by the large proportion of coal hauled on the branches of the Pennsylvania Railroad which does not come to New York, and also by the greater concentration of business (see line 29) caused by the less number of city stations (see line 5), and the same reasons cause the differences shown on line 31.

Terminal Works and Business of the New York, Lake Erie & Western Railroad.

The business of this road extends over many branches and connections throughout the Western states and over a large part of the state of New York, and also into the coal and oil regions of Pennsylvania.

Its terminal stations in New Jersey are : The distributing yard, located just west of the tunnel through Bergen Hill ; the principal yard and freight and passenger stations and docks in Jersey City, on the west bank of the Hudson River, opposite Canal street, New York, which is $1\frac{3}{4}$ miles north of the Battery ; the coal, oil, live stock and export provision depots and docks at Weehawken, opposite Thirtieth street, New York, about $3\frac{1}{2}$ miles north of the Battery.

In New York city are : The flour station on the East River, the principal city freight and passenger station at the foot of Chambers street on the Hudson River ; the uptown freight and passenger station at the foot of West Twenty-third street.

The Brooklyn station is in Williamsburg, near the piers used by the other railroads.

BERGEN YARD.—This yard is located partly in the entrance cut at the west approach of Bergen Tunnel and partly on a light bank over the Hackensack Meadows, and is crossed overhead by the New York, Susquehanna & Western Railroad by a two-span bridge about one-quarter of the whole length west of the tunnel. The yard is simply a series of sidings parallel to the main tracks, the east-bound yard on the south next the east-bound track consisting of seven tracks, and the west-bound on the north next the west-bound track of five tracks. West of the bridge above mentioned the yard is about one mile long, and the sidings are long and with few cross-overs. East of the bridge the yard is about three-eighths of a mile long and each siding holds about the number of cars generally sent to Jersey City in a train. The roundhouse and coal-pockets for the road and yard engines are situated just south of the eastern yard. There are 18 miles of available track in the sidings of both yards.

The through fast freight trains for the West are frequently made up in this yard, and the east-bound trains are sorted here in a general way for destination. It is also a storing yard when the Jersey City and Weehawken yards are full, and as it is a union yard for the different branches and connections of the Eastern Division much work is necessarily done here. There are 4 engines in use during the day and 3 at night ; the best have 3 pairs of drivers and 1 pair of forward trucks, with tender. They weigh 37 tons, with 31 tons on the drivers.

There are 15 men employed here constantly on maintenance of way.

JERSEY CITY TERMINUS.—This yard (see Plate A) has been developed as the business increased. The city streets all cross at grade, and the four between Grove street and the tunnel are guarded by flagmen and portcullis gates.

The car repair sheds and shops of this division are just west of Grove street. East of Grove street there are 45 acres in the whole property to the bulkhead. There are about 25 miles of available sidings in this yard, of which 14 miles are used on east-bound, 8 miles on west-bound, and 3 miles on passenger business. The yard engines used in this and the Bergen yard are broad-gauge ; hence the tracks are all three-rail tracks, requiring additional expense in maintenance. (The third rail is now being removed from the yard, and all the tracks in it will hereafter be of standard gauge only.) The freight houses are ordinary one-story sheds ; the covered area on east-bound business is 142,000 square feet, on west-bound 64,000 square feet. The general arrangement of business is sufficiently indicated on the plan.

The working force in the yard is 9 engines during the day and 4 at night, with 70 train and yard men during the day and 30 at night, moving from 400 to 600 cars of all kinds each way a day.

There are 25 men on maintenance of track employed in this yard

The trains moved on this division are heavy, the engines very large and powerful and the grades steep ; hence not more than 8 per cent. of the cost of maintenance of cars is chargeable to station work.

With the exception of its location (which necessitates the shifting of all the grain cars across the passenger tracks), the grain elevator is an excellent example of the economical results arising from the application of classification and of the use of machinery to the work of handling freight. It was built and is operated by private parties. 16,000,000 bushels of grain were delivered by this railroad in 1883.

The pier is extended beyond the elevator for the purpose of transferring grain directly from the cars to lighters, in case it is not necessary to store it in the elevator.

In the small building marked *A* is an elevator, by means of which grain is raised from boats and transferred by belt conveyors into the main elevator building. In the latter there are ten legs, and the grain is raised from the cars on one track at a time, each track holding ten cars. When emptied, the yard engine backs the loaded cars in, thus pushing the empty cars out on the pier ; hence a shift is only made when the pier tracks are full, thus economizing time.

Two yard engines are employed on this work for an ordinary day's work of 150 cars ; 310 cars of grain have been handled here in a day, however, requiring three yard engines to move them.

The building is well lighted and arranged. It is furnished with two upright low-pressure beam engines, one in use and one in reserve. They are supplied with a very economical cut-off, and the boilers are well set and the draft thoroughly regulated by an effective damper, and the consumption of coal is hardly half that at other well-arranged elevators.

WEEHAWKEN TERMINUS.—A branch track starting from the main line just east of the tunnel, and running north about three miles (crossing the Delaware, Lackawanna & Western Railroad under grade), leads to the Weehawken docks, on the Hudson River. This property has a frontage of 2,400 ft. on the river and an average width of 900 ft. from the present water line, making 50 acres of land, of which 10 acres are occupied by the stock yards and 10 acres by the oil works.

The bulkhead has not been built, and the tracks run to the piers over trestle-work. Altogether outside of the oil works there are 8 miles of track and sidings.

The northernmost pier, 650 ft. long and 70 ft. wide, is covered by a one-story shed used for the transfer of west-bound freight from lighters to cars. South of this is a slip 150 ft. wide and then a pier 680 ft. long and 70 ft. wide, covered by a two-story shed, in which east-bound provisions of all kinds are handled, mostly for export.

The freight for the second floor (mostly flour in bags) is raised by two endless-chain automatic elevators (patented) like those at the Sixtieth Street station of the New York Central Railroad. Here, however, each is worked by a small independent engine. The bags, etc., of flour are delivered to the lighters from the second floor by chutes, which are simply plank troughs suspended at the upper end from an opening in the second floor, leading out of the gangway door and running to the deck of the boat. The lower part is hinged to make it adjustable, and it is all raised and lowered by a block and fall. This appliance saves all labor on the first floor, and is a very simple and effective labor-saving arrangement. About 1,670,000 barrels of flour were delivered by this railroad in 1883.

Similar chutes, constructed of slats of half-round iron laid in a parabolic curve (steep at the upper end and nearly level at the

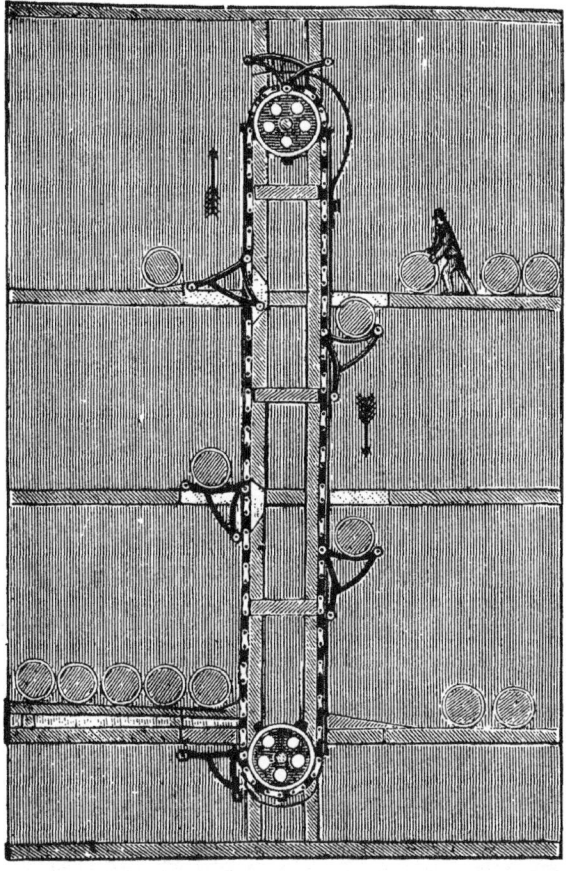

lower end), are frequently seen in warehouses in the city for lowering all kinds of freight from the street sidewalk to the elevator in the middle of the cellars.

The construction of this shed is shown in the cut of Pier B ; the doors are hung and slide on the outside of the building, which is a good arrangement.

South of this pier is a slip 200 ft. wide to a proposed pier not

Oversized Foldout

yet begun, 720 ft. long and 80 ft. wide. Facing this slip is a three-story cold-storage provision warehouse. The freight, mostly barrels, is moved by another form of endless-chain elevator (patented), called the Ruddell elevator [see illustration] which both lowers and raises at the same time. Most of the freight, however, is lowered by chutes. This elevator can also be used for handling freight packed in bags, bales and boxes, though these latter modes of packing require somewhat more labor.

The business at the oil works operated by the Standard Oil Co. is barreling and shipping oil ; there are three piers here.

The stock-yards have never been wholly in use, but are located on high, well-drained land 400 ft. from the river, and are very well built. Lying adjacent to this property, on the north, are the coal piers of the Delaware & Hudson Canal Co., and on the south those of the Pennsylvania Coal Co., and, in fact, all the piers at this station are operated by independent corporations and firms, and the railroad company only moves the cars. There are three engines employed here and in running to and from Bergen yard, moving between 250 and 400 cars of all kinds a day each way.

IN NEW YORK CITY.—Flour Pier on East River.—This is next to the New York Central & Hudson River Railroad pier, a third of a mile north of the Battery. It is a narrow pier, covered with a shed, one-half of which is used for a roadway and one-half for storing flour. The freight is moved to it in lighters and barges.

General Freight Station on the Hudson River is at the foot of Chambers street, 1¼ miles north of the Battery. The freight sheds here have a frontage of 400 ft. on West street, as there are two piers, each 100 ft. wide at the bulkheads, with a slip 200 ft. wide between them.

The construction of the sheds is shown in the illustration. They are well lighted and kept neat.

The piers are very large and roomy ; they are 575 ft. long from the bulkhead line.

A wagon way, 20 ft. wide, extends all the way around next the water, and the east-bound freight is unloaded from the cars on the floats and piled in the centre. A large cheese business is carried on here.

The west-bound freight is hauled partly on the piers and partly on the bulkhead.

There is a floating sorting shed, 50 ft. wide, along the whole length of the bulkhead, 200 ft., which breaks the difference in level between the floats and the bulkhead, caused by the changes in tide and load. This floating shed is in addition to the receiving shed, and 50 ft. wide on the bulkhead.

The weighing of west-bound freight is done on small movable platform scales, which are run to the dray, and the freight is weighed alone, and not on a hand truck. The total covered area is 124,500 square feet.

The Twenty-third Street Station is about three miles north of the Battery. This is a pier about 150 ft. long and 50 ft. wide, used for shipping west-bound freight from the up-town manufacturing districts. The freight is loaded on barges and rehandled at Jersey City.

WILLIAMSBURGH STATION.—The Brooklyn business of this railroad, unlike that of the others, is done by means of car floats. The cars are transferred from the floats over a transfer bridge at the Williamsburgh docks by a dummy engine and run across an important city street to a station. Considerable east-bound freight—vegetables, etc.—is delivered here, and the west-bound sugar from the refineries is loaded directly on the cars, instead of on the barges. Small lots, however, must be transferred at Jersey City to other cars.

All lighterage is done by this company with its own equipment.

Terminal Works and Business of the Delaware, Lackawanna & Western Railroad.

Although the principal business of this company is the transportation of anthracite coal from the Lackawanna district of the Pennsylvania coal fields, it has necessarily enlarged the character of its business by the construction of an independent double-track railroad to Buffalo, where it makes a western connection to Chicago, principally over the New York, Chicago & St. Louis Railroad. It operates also a line to Oswego, on Lake Ontario, and over it and several other branches, has direct connections to some of the rich and fertile districts of the central part of the State of New York. It remains, however, in its operation as far as possible only a transportation company, its whole business ending at the station (shown on Plate A) at Hoboken, on the west side of the Hudson River, about opposite Christopher street, New York, 2¼ miles north of the Battery.

The handling of the miscellaneous freight at this station, the lighterage to and from New York, and the handling in the city are all done under a contract with a private firm ; hence, in addition to the necessary work of moving cars in the yard, the principal work done directly by this company is simply the handling of the coal.

Like the Pennsylvania and Erie Railroads, this railroad has a yard on the Hackensack Meadows (called the Secaucus Yard), but it is a small one, being simply a series of sidings parallel to the main line, making in all about six miles of track. Thence the grade of the road ascends 26 feet to the mile to the tunnel through Bergen Hill, which is entered at about the same point as the Erie Railway, but on a considerably higher level and in a more northerly direction. The eastern portal of this tunnel is only 1,600 ft. from the beginning of the yard, and, as the grade is high, all the city streets are crossed overhead by substantial iron bridges.

The northerly part of the yard above the ship canal is devoted to the passenger, local freight and iron business, and is now being rebuilt according to the plan. There are 9 miles of track in the passenger yard and 11 miles of track in the freight yard. Five yard engines are employed here. The southern part of the yard has been lately built and regularly graded, and all the tracks are in excellent line and surface, and of new material. There are 34 miles of track, of which about 23 miles are in the coal yards and docks. Four engines are used in the coal yard and three in the through freight yard.

Pier 5, running by the side of the long ship canal, carries a series of high level trestle tracks, which run to it from the overhead bridge across the street. The coal runs from the dump cars by chutes into the vessels or is stocked on the pier beneath. It is devoted to the business of the N. Y., S. & W. R. R.

Piers 6, 7, 8, 9 and 10 are built in a general way on the plan indicated on Plate B. The loaded cars are hoisted by an endless wire rope up a steep inclined plane from the tracks in the yard to the elevated trestle work on the piers, and the coal is dumped into the bins and thence into the vessels. The empty cars are then run by gravity down a longer inclined trestle work track in the yard ; as shown on the plan, the "empty" tracks are sometimes in the centre and sometimes on the sides of the pier; the newest and best-arranged pier is No. 10. The inclined planes on all these "gravity" piers are furnished with "dogs," one pair to each bent. They are two sticks of timber (about 4 in. × 8 in), hung on an axle, which is a heavy bar of round iron running across the plane, with its ends set into the stringers on each side. The lower and longer ends of the "dog" rest on the cap below, and the short upper end projects far enough above the rail to catch the axles of the cars. As a car is hauled up the plane, each axle scrapes along the top edges of the "dogs," and thus lowers the upper ends and passes on. The "dogs" then—as the lower ends are the heavier—return to their original position, and in case of accident the upper ends of the "dogs" catch the axle of the car, and thus prevent it from running down the plane.

The coal is hauled generally in small four-wheeled dump cars, occupying about 13 feet in length of train weighing 7,500 lbs. and carrying about 12,000 lbs. of coal. Gondola cars with hoppers are also used, occupying 28 feet in a train weighing 19,500 lbs. and carrying 40,000 lbs. of coal.

The east-bound road engines haul 100 loaded four-wheeled cars in a train to Secaucus yard, and the train is there divided, 60 cars being hauled through the tunnel by the road engine and 40 by a "tunnel engine." The engines are uncoupled at the head of the yard, and the train of cars runs by gravity down the grade on the receiving tracks, and the engines are turned on the turntable "A," and haul empty cars back.

The cars on arrival are immediately inspected, the boxes filled, and the date of arrival marked with white chalk on each car. The yard engine then hauls them back up the grade, and with the grade descending in the direction of the work sorts the cars.

Piers 6, 7, 8 and 9 are devoted to the business of the agents of different mines, generally two consignees on a pier. Each agent keeps separate and sells independently the coal from each mine, making in all some 30 different consignments; consequently, they must be separated in the yard, and also each mine ships several different sizes of coal, which must also be separated in order to do the work on the piers regularly and systematically; and therefore the yard for each of these piers is adm'rably designed for this work of sorting into a series of small yards, as shown in the plan.

The yard of No. 10 indicates a different arrangement of business. The coal handled on this pier is mined entirely by the Scranton Coal Co., which classes the product of all its mines alike and does not separate them. Therefore, the sorting of this coal is simply the necessary separation of the sizes, which is done at Port Morris yard, about 30 miles to the west, and hence the trains arrive in the Hoboken yard assorted in sizes, and the only yard work needed is to place the cars so that they can be hauled up on the plane.

In winter two of the small cars (in summer generally three) are hooked by a chain to a link in a wire cable of $1\frac{1}{4}$ in. diameter, which runs over a sheave wheel at each end of the plane to the drum below. Both drums—one under each track—are fastened to the same shaft and revolve in the same direction, but the cables being wound in opposite directions, the cars are raised on one plane at a time. The drum shaft is geared directly to the driving shaft of a pair of 16×30 in. cylinder horizontal engines, which, with the boilers, are operated by one man, and use about $1\frac{1}{2}$ tons of coal in a day of 10 hours.

On arriving at the head of the plane, the cars immediately pass over the scales and are weighed, and they are then easily placed at any bin on the pier, as the tracks are well arranged.

The bins are arranged as shown on the plan; they are lined with sheet iron, and the coal is dumped from the cars, runs over the bar screens (the sizes of which are stated), and thence runs over the iron apron into the vessel. These aprons are hinged at the trestle end, and are raised and lowered by means of chains running to an ordinary hand drum gearing at the top. The dust and screenings are wheeled back on the pier and shipped separately. The bins are of different sizes, and the aprons at different heights to accommodate the different vessels. The sailing vessels running to Boston and other points on the coast carry from 700 to 800 tons, and when they are empty the coal is run into them from the high bins. The coal for New York City is carried in canal boats of 230 to 250 tons capacity, and with them the larger and deeper bins are used. These latter bins will hold 50 tons, and hence the movement of the cars need not wait on the work of "trimming" or spreading the load and moving the boats.

The dumping of the cars (which is done by opening the hinged doors in the bottom) and their movement on the pier is done by men employed by the company. Thirty-five men on Pier 10 can handle 3,000 tons in a day of 10 hours, for there is but little shoveling required, either in the gondola hopper cars or the small dump cars.

At the river end of Pier No. 10 is a coaling station for tug boats. The coal is dumped directly on the dock and is delivered to the boats by a contrivance worth mentioning : It is a small car, carrying a sheet-iron hopper, holding about a ton of coal, which is weighed by scales rigged on the car itself ; by this means the coal, wherever it may be, is weighed immediately and run to its destination. Its possible application to other work is the reason this car is noted here. Commercially speaking, the most active time in the coal trade is in the fall and spring of the year ; in summer the coal is not so quickly sold, but it is the best season of the year for its mining. Therefore, during the summer much more coal arrives at the docks than is shipped from them, and consequently it must be stocked. This is done in great piles running back from the bulkhead, sometimes 400 ft. long and 25 ft. high, and in the autumn, when this coal is shipped, the vessels lie at the bulkhead and the coal is wheeled to them in wheelbarrows. Each wheelbarrow delivers 224 lbs. of coal, which is screened, loaded and wheeled by hand and the weight tested and corrected on a small platform scales, placed wherever convenient. If cars such as are mentioned above could be applied to the work of moving stocked coal, their use would lead to considerable economy in the work of handling coal in certain conditions of the trade.

It is evident that the chief advantage in expense of operating which the coal-carrying road has over a road doing a general business is in the handling of the freight, for while the proportion of paying to dead load per car is much greater—perhaps twice— in the case of a coal car than in a merchandise car, still the coal car is always hauled back empty and also it runs back against the grade of the road, hence, although its movement is very prompt and regular, its practical working and paying capacity is diminished to perhaps one half of what appears on the face.

Terminal Works of the New York, West Shore & Buffalo and New York, Ontario & Western Railways at New York.

The West Shore Railway runs east from Buffalo (where it connects with the Grand Trunk Railway and its Western system) by following the general line of the N. Y. C. & H. R. R. across the State of New York, though on opposite sides of the principal streams ; and the Ontario & Western Railway runs in a southeasterly direction, crossing the mountains of Sullivan and Delaware counties, from Oswego, on Lake Ontario.

They connect about 50 miles north of New York at Cornwall-on-

Oversized Foldout

Oversized Foldout

the-Hudson, and run into New Jersey back of the Palisades, and end in one union terminal station at Weehawken, N. J., on the west bank of the Hudson River, opposite Fiftieth street, New York, 5 miles north of the Battery.

About two miles to the west, near the Hackensack Meadows, but on high, well drained land, is the New Durham yard for sorting and storing trains. This consists of a series of 20 or more sidings, parallel to and on one side of the main line. Most of these sidings are about 3,000 ft. long, and extend altogether a mile in length. The yard contains about 22 miles of available track when finished. Between this yard and the Weehawken terminus is the tunnel, nearly one mile long, under Union Hill. The river side of this hill is a steep, rocky bluff, forming the beginning of the Palisades, and the eastern portal of the tunnel is only 800 ft. back from the original water line of the river. The strip of land of about that width, extending for nearly 6,800 feet along the river, was laid out as shown on the plan, and the construction work, begun in 1881, is still being carried on to some extent.

As the line of the bulkhead was fixed (a portion of the way) 300 feet back from the original water line, a canal was dredged from the river, and the dredging machines were then turned and a trench was excavated for the cribwork, from 30 to 40 feet in height, which forms the bulkhead.

The yard was filled in with good material and some ashes behind the bulkhead, but the rocky bottom dipped so rapidly toward the river that considerable trouble was caused by the movement of the silt as it was loaded with the new material.

The piers are 200 feet wide, which necessitated the style of construction of the two-story freight sheds shown on the plan.

The yard engines used here are tank locomotives, weighing complete 50 tons, all on three pairs of drivers.

In New York City: These roads have four freight stations on the Hudson River: A flour station on Pier No. 1 at the Battery, and the principal general freight station on Pier No. 5, a short distance north, half of which is used by the Pennsylvania Railroad; and another at Harrison street, near the dry-goods district, where west-bound freight is loaded on a barge.

The up-town station is at the foot of Thirty-sixth street. This is the only station in New York City at which cars from the New Jersey shore are run over transfer bridges from the car floats to tracks in the city. This enabled the establishment of freight houses on the city streets and allows the convenient and direct transfer of some freight between the cars and drays. The eastbound freight handled here is largely hay and provisions, and the west-bound freight miscellaneous manufactures.

These companies own and operate their own lighterage equipment.

New Jersey Central Railroad.

This railroad is operated by the Philadelphia & Reading R. R. Co., and by this connection its business extends to Philadelphia and throughout most of Northeastern and into Central Pennsylvania, and especially into the anthracite coal fields of Schuylkill, Lehigh and Luzerne counties.

Its principal termini on the New Jersey Shore are : The general freight and passenger station and yard at Communipaw, about opposite the Battery, and the coal yards and piers at Bergen Point, or Port Johnson, and also at Elizabethport, the former opposite the north end of Staten Island, and the latter just below the entrance of Newark Bay, on the Kill von Kull.

The approach of this railroad to New York is from the south crossing, Newark Bay, avoiding Bergen Hill, and is altogether in open and level country.

The yard at Communipaw, Jersey City, is long and level, and an elevated track on the coal dock here at the south of the yard is approached by a steep grade on trestle-work operated by a locomotive which pushes up about 20 small cars. A large business is done here in coaling coastwise steamers and tugs, and coal is also hauled from this yard in wagons over the ferry to supply the southern part of New York City.

The works at Bergen Point or Port Johnson are chiefly devoted to handling the coal mined by the Lehigh & Wilkesbarre Coal Co. The coal is handled in much the same way as at Hoboken, except that the cars are delivered on the high trestles on the piers directly by the locomotives, the location allowing this without the use of heavy grades.

The stocked coal, however, after being dumped from the high trestle for storage, is hauled up a heavy grade, being reloaded on the standard cars at about 6 ft. above the level of the bulkhead, and hauled by locomotives up into the yard and thence to the pier, being weighed, dumped and screened as though it came directly from the mines.

Elizabethport is the old coal depot, where there are several short piers on which the Schuylkill and Luzerne coal is handled in the same or similar way as at Bergen Point.

This company has a general freight station at the foot of Liberty street, New York, on the Hudson River docks, operated in the usual way by means of car floats.

Lehigh Valley Railroad.

The freight business of this railroad enters the port by way of the Easton & Amboy Railroad, with a terminus on the Kill von Kull at Perth Amboy.

It carries on a large coal transportation business from the Lehigh Valley and Wilkesbarre regions. This company has a general freight station in New York on the Hudson River, on Pier No. 2, near the Battery.

Its coal docks and piers at Perth Amboy are similar to the others mentioned, except that the approach is on a high level, and the cars are delivered on the high trestle tracks on the piers by gravity, the shifting and movement of empty cars being done by horses.

Here also are located the great storage grounds for "stocking" coal. The cars, both in-bound loaded and out-bound empty, are moved entirely by gravity over light trestle work, 20 or 30 ft. high, above the flat lands lying between the hills on which the road is located and the water. About 15 acres of land have been covered with bins from 20 to 30 ft. deep, divided by timber walls, and holding about 1,000 tons each, and altogether storing about 250,000 tons of coal, which is dumped from the high level trestle tracks. Underneath each row of bins is a tunnel into which are run trains of standard four-wheeled cars, handled by powerful tank locomotives, similar to a mine locomotive. The tunnels were open cuts in the gradually sloping ground, and were lined with timber, like a mine gallery.

The coal is loaded into the cars from the bins without shoveling through trap-doors in the bottom of the bins, as is generally done in an anthracite mine from the "breasts."

The loaded cars are hauled up a heavy grade and handled in the usual way on the piers.

This large storage capacity enables this company to operate its mines and railroad regularly, thus giving steady work to the men it employs.

Without information and figures to determine otherwise, it would seem that the best arrangement for the terminal works of a coal transporting railroad would be a combination of a well-planned sorting yard with the Hoboken method of delivering and handling and the Perth Amboy method of storing, and the site which would naturally allow of this arrangement would be preferable to others.

New York, New Haven & Hartford Railroad and New York & Harlem Railroad.

The through Boston and Eastern freight is handled at Pier 50, foot of Montgomery street, East River ($1\frac{1}{2}$ miles north of the Battery), by means of car floats running between that pier and the transfer on the Harlem River.

The local freight of both the New Haven and Harlem Railroads is handled at a union station bounded by Centre, White, Elm and Franklin streets. It is a brick building, built about 40 years ago, with factories on the upper floors.

The cars are moved night and day between here and the Grand Central Depot on Forty-second street, $2\frac{3}{4}$ miles north, by horses. The movement of freight at this station is prompt, 100 cars being handled here daily on a space about 200 ft. square, containing 8 tracks and the necessary platforms.

New York City & Northern Railroad.

This railroad has a direct connection with the New York & New England Railroad. Its business is done by means of car floats between its transfer station on the Harlem River at High Bridge, and its city station at Pier 40, East River, foot of Pike street, $1\frac{1}{4}$ miles north of the Battery.

Long Island Railroad.

This railroad extends throughout Long Island. Its principal in-bound freight is the product of "truck" farms, and its only freight station in the city, operated by car floats from Hunter's Point, is at Pier 35, East River, foot of Catharine street, 1 mile north of the Battery. Two thousand barrels of vegetables are handled here in a night.

Most sincere thanks to the officers and men of all the different roads must be added to these very incomplete notes, for the kindness and readiness with which the information desired has invariably been furnished.

GENERAL SUMMARY.

It is seen that there are two general systems of terminal work illustrated at New York—one in which separate stations and yards are used for local and for through freight, and as far as possible for car-load lots, as on the Pennsylvania Railroad, and the other at which all freight is handled at a common station and sorted, both in-bound and out-bound, in one great terminal yard like the Sixtieth Street Yard of the New York Central & Hudson River Railroad.

While the first system is probably quicker in its operation, the second is sometimes more convenient; but what is most striking in both systems, is the amount of work and room expended by the railroads for very uncertain and irregular compensation.

The description of the works of the New York Central & Hudson River Railroad shows the great amount of room occupied, and, owing to competition among the railroad companies, it is the case with all the other roads, in handling east-bound freight (such as flour, cheese and many other kinds of merchandise), and that this item of room and storage in a city like New York leads to great expense both in itself and in the additional labor required in its operation. The details of this work are certainly worthy of serious consideration, for it is well established that one of the most important principles in the economical operation of railroads is the care of those little things which are thousands of times repeated in practice.

The description of the Pennsylvania Railroad work shows the inconvenience of operating works located on narrow piers at tidewater.

The description of the D., L. & W. R. R. terminal work is intended to show the advantage of designing the yard for the work to be done in it (as is also shown in the Sixtieth Street Yard of the N. Y. C. & H. R. R. R.), and also the advantage of having works specially devoted to one kind of business, insuring promptness and system, and possibly leading to the use of machinery.

This consideration becomes important, as in the transportation business, especially of through freight, the proportion of " staple" freight shipped in car-load lots seems to be increasing, and its separation and classification will be constantly more closely watched.

In the description of the Erie R. R. works, some interesting labor-saving appliances are mentioned, and the sketch of the works of the West Shore Railway is given chiefly to show their location and arrangement; while the whole is intended to emphasize the intimate connection between the work and expenses in the yard and those in the freight house, as distinguished from those on the road.

That these works have been located over a large area is natural, on account of the great extent of available water-front; but it would seem that the work, as a whole, can only be cheapened by rearranging and concentrating it, and by applying system and promptness throughout; and as it must always be made convenient to the merchants, much study and consultation will be necessary before any general permanent plan can be determined, in case it should ever be considered desirable.

The accompanying table is an unofficial approximate estimate of the actual capital represented in the terminal work of moving and handling freight by the trunk line railroads at the port of New York.

It includes the work of handling coal on the Delaware, Lackawanna & Western Railroad, but on no other, and only includes a small part of the expenses of handling and lighterage of grain, oil and live stock, and none of the expenses of clerical work and management on any of the roads.

The only direct return received from the merchants by these railroad companies for this work, the plant of which represents an aggregate actual capital of at least $35,000,000, and the power an annual expenditure of at least $3,500,000, are the charges collected for long-distance lighterage.

Assuming 6 per cent. interest, this shows a total annual expense of $5,500,000, and taking into account clerk hire, management, repairs, taxes, light, stationery, insurance and all other expenses, the total is probably not far from $10,000,000, or an average burden on each road of $2,000,000 every year.

Oversized Foldout

TABULAR SUMMARY OF THE RAILROAD FACILITIES FOR HANDLING FREIGHT AT THE PORT OF NEW YORK.

Name of Road.	Plant.										Power.	
	Fixed.						Locomotive.					
	Total Track in all Yards.	Termini on Hudson River.					Yard Engines.	Propellers.	Lighters.	Average Laborers, etc., employed daily at Yards, Stations and Lighters.	Average Coal used daily.	
		Track in Yards.	Area of Yards, Ex. of Piers.	Area of Piers.	Covered Floor Area.	New York City Sta's Covered Floor Area.						
	Miles.	Miles.	As.	Sq. ft.	Sq. ft.	Sq. ft.	No.	No.	No.	No.	Tons.	
N. Y. C. & H. R. R. R.	28	28	83	450,000	350,000	350,000	14	12	40	1,300	110	
Penna. R. R.	39	20	71	300,000	360,000	290,000	15	16	80	1,300	120	
N. Y., L. E. & W. R. R.	49	30	70	250,000	300,000	150,000	16	8	55	1,000	100	
D. L. & W. R. R.	50	44	74	600,000	a 540,000	b	15	b	b	b 300	b 50	
N.Y., W. S. & B. Ry. & N. Y., O. & W. Ry.	34	12	80	c 600,000	450,000	100,000	d 9	8	55	800	70	
Total	200	134	378	2,200,000	e 2,000,000	890,000	69	44	230	4,700	450	
Cost per unit, dollars	10.000	....	52.000	1.00	0.80	f 6.00	8.700	25.000	9.000	2.00 @ 6 per cent.	4.00 @ 6 per cent.	
Representing millions of dollars capital	2.000	....	g 20.000	2.200	1.600	5.400	0.600	1.100	2.100	47.000	9.000	

a. Includes coal trestles. *b.* None of the expenses of handling and lighterage of miscellaneous freight on this road are included, as that work is done by contract. *c.* Proposed total, 1,500,000 sq. ft. *d.* Most of the freight on these roads comes in large lots, hence there is less sorting of cars required in the yards than would be required otherwise. *e.* Includes area of both 1st and 2d floors, but not the track room. *f.* Includes both land and structures. *g.* Includes land grading, etc., at all yards and stations except in the city proper.

Terminal work in general, then, is the connection between the operations of simple transportation and those of sale and delivery, and if it were found possible in the latter to adopt the rule of giving at the time of shipment of all freight its specific destination (a warehouse, storehouse or factory, as the case may be, and not a railroad freight house), it would ultimately lead to greater promptness in the work of handling, which would undoubtedly prove beneficial to both the merchants and the railroad companies.

GENERAL CONCLUSIONS.

It would seem that the subject of terminal work is well worthy of study in this country. In large cities, and especially in New York, it appears to be the key to the solution of many of the problems relating to transportation, and the principles on which it is conducted control the business of production and sale in some of the great industries of the country.

It may be true that in certain stages of development the competition of similar interests which are naturally situated alike is most conducive to the public good ; but after these individual interests have proved their worth and become firmly established, their proper and regular growth becomes a part of the good of the State, and is inseparably connected with its progress. At such times the indiscriminate application of the principal of competition sometimes results, as in this case, in one industry bearing the burdens which legitimately belong to others. There will probably be presented, some time in the future, then, the following question : How can the terminal work at New York best be consolidated into a well-regulated and progressive combination ?

This combination would seem to be best regulated by a law which should enforce a full, clear, detailed public statement of accounts ; and, with this fundamental principle established, there need be little fear of serious abuses in its management. This system of accounts could depend for one thing upon a thoroughly classified diary of all kinds of labor and material furnished, and to what special freight and work applied.

The progressive and effective operation, resting as it should on the principle that the foundation of the economical handling of freight is *promptness*, is a complicated question, which can only be determined after thorough study and experiment. It can be said, however, that New York, by its location, is peculiarly fitted for the establishment of great public works for this purpose. The great transportation companies possibly might themselves form a Union Terminal Company, which could establish a connecting railroad and one or more union terminal yards on the Hackensack Meadows, where most of the freight, both in-bound and out-bound, could be thoroughly and systematically sorted according to its character and destination, thereby greatly reducing and consolidating the present termini on the Hudson River. These yards could be designed, perhaps, after the plan of some of the great English gravity yards, as may be seen illustrated in Volume XLI. of Transactions of the Institution of Civil Engineers for 1875. A rough sketch of a yard, copied mostly from the Sixtieth Street and Hoboken Yards, is given in the accompanying cut, but it does not include the English system of secondary yards, which might be advantageously applied to the sorting of local freight trains. In connection with this might be established, especially for goods for local supply and storage and interior shipments, a few great depots in the city, and again its peculiar location seems to make this possible. The main part of the city is on an island about ten miles long and only two miles wide ; hence its growth is confined and is mostly in one direction, and, as only a certain number of persons can live on an acre of ground, the amount and location of this growth can be determined. Certain portions of the city have been and can be, with much certainty, set apart for factories, others for wholesale and retail business, and others for dwellings, and around the whole are deep waters, which are navigable even during the severe winters. The most populous and busy part of the city is naturally divided into four districts, being respectively above and below Fourteenth Street on the east and on the west, and hence the number of depots need not probably be more than six. At these depots the business of handling certain freight could be separated from the business of storage, which could be put on a paying basis, while the handling might be done largely by machinery, one suggestion in regard to which is shown in the accompanying cut.

The conveyers there proposed would be constructed like a horse-tread-mill, flush with and forming a part of the floor about 4 or 5 feet wide, propelled slowly by steam machinery, and controlled by a brake. If a similar contrivance could be applied to out-bound freight on the car floats, it would introduce both economy and system into the work, but its practical application to any work of the kind can only be determined by experiment.

The principle, however, of continuous vertical elevators, combined with continuous horizontal conveyers, weighing and automatically recording the number of pieces at the same time the freight is moved, may prove applicable to the handling of freight, both bulk and merchandise, in many cases ; in unloading vessels as well as in freight houses and on docks.

The hauling in the city also might be properly regulated and more systematically carried on, thus adding economy, convenience and promptness to the work of the merchants, and the work of weighing miscellaneous freight perhaps done more economically than at present.

Improvements might also be made in the methods of handling coal, as may be seen in the operation of handling a considerable part of the coal supply of New England.

After good information on all these subjects has been obtained, a general plan could be determined, which would probably give better results than to adhere to the present plan of allowing each road to answer the questions arising each day for itself alone ; hence, whatever may be the value of these suggestions, it can be expected that this whole question in its broadest form will ultimately receive the attention of some practical men, and that the combined efforts of a Railroad President, a General Superintendent, a General Freight Agent, a Chief Engineer, a Mechanical Engineer and a Railroad Auditor, working in co-operation with the merchants, will finally result in decisive improvement in this work.

Even if the radical changes proposed above should be found impracticable, some useful modifications of the present arrangements can probably be agreed upon ; and with this end in view it would seem proper to determine as correctly as possible the approximate cost, both to the merchants and to the railroad companies, of handling and storing different kinds of freight by the present methods, investigating separately the important articles of commerce, such as grain, flour and provisions, and classifying general merchandise according to the different modes of packing and handling.

It may be well to state in closing these notes, that the faith in their value arises not so much from a belief in their intrinsic worth as from the opinion that, at least in portions of this country, the era of rapid railroad construction is steadily giving way to the era of thoughtful railroad improvement, and that, whatever interest they may excite will largely be due to an appreciation of this fact ; and also that there is probably no one thing which would be more likely to give stability to the values of American railroad properties than the striking example which would be set by the adoption of a broad-minded, well-considered plan for the terminal work at New York.

Schedule and Explanation

OF THE ACCOMPANYING

MAP OF NEW YORK CITY AND SURROUNDINGS.

The City of New York is divided into six districts, as follows:

District No. 1, or Southwest.—All of the city south of Fourteenth street and west of the Bowery, and also all south of Liberty street from river to river.

District No. 2, or Southeast.—All south of Fourteenth street to Liberty street and east of the Bowery.

District No. 3, or Northwest.—All north of Fourteenth street to Eighty-sixth street and west of Sixth avenue.

District No. 4, or Northeast.—All north of Fourteenth street to Eighty-sixth street and east of Sixth avenue.

District No. 5, or Harlem.—All of the city north of East and West Eighty-sixth street to Harlem River.

District No. 6, or Annexed.—All of the city north of Harlem River to Westchester County.

Property colored red shows location of railroad termini.

Property colored blue shows location of wholesale dealers in manufactures.

Property colored yellow shows location of wholesale dealers in food.

Property colored black shows location of markets and storehouses.

TABULAR STATEMENT OF POPULATION.

District No.	Area, acres.	Estimated average population per acre. Y'r '85.	Y'r '95.	Estimated total population. Year 1885.	Year 1895.
1	1,302	181	190	236,000	247,000
2	1,106	321	325	353,000	360,000
3	2,322	124	200	288,000	464,000
4	2,342	147	200	344,000	468,000
Total south of 86th st.	7,072	172	*217	1,221,000	1,539,000
5	5,504	22		123,000	
6	12,317	4		52,000	
Grand total	24,893	56		1,396,000	

* This is about the present average population of the Twentieth Ward.

ESTIMATED POPULATION OF SURROUNDING CITIES.

Brooklyn.

District.	Area, acres.	Population 1885. Average per acre.	Total.
Greenpoint district	729	50	36,000
Williamsburgh district	6,983	46	317,000
Central Brooklyn	3,509	71	248,000
South Brooklyn	2,086	23	50,000
Total	13,307	49	651,000

In New Jersey.

Jersey City, Hoboken and adjacent towns	160,000
Newark and adjacent towns	160,000
Total	320,000

APPROXIMATE ESTIMATE OF LOCAL SUPPLY OF NEW YORK CITY.

Tabular statement of the average daily tonnage of freight delivered direct to consumers south of Eighty-sixth street.

In the Year 1885.

From 14th st.	West side.		East side.		Total.	
	Food, clothing, etc.	Coal.	Food, clothing, etc.	Coal.	Food, clothing, etc.	Coal.
South	1,200	2,500	1,000	2,500	2,200	5,000
North	1,000	2,000	900	2,200	1,900	4,200
Total	**2,200**	**4,500**	**1,900**	**4,700**	**4,100**	**9.200**
			In the Year 1895.			
South	1,250	2,700	1,000	2,800	2,250	5,500
North	1,750	3,300	1,200	3,200	2,950	6,500
Total	**3,000**	**6,000**	**2,200**	**6,000**	**5,200**	**12,000**

Oversized Foldout

$\frac{M}{150}$

Printed in Dunstable, United Kingdom